IN GOD'S WOMB

IN GOD'S WOMB

A Spiritual Memoir

EDWINA GATELEY

Maryknoll, New York 10545

Second Printing, February 2011

Founded in 1970, Orbis Books endeavors to publish works that enlighten the mind, nourish the spirit, and challenge the conscience. The publishing arm of the Maryknoll Fathers and Brothers, Orbis seeks to explore the global dimensions of the Christian faith and mission, to invite dialogue with diverse cultures and religious traditions, and to serve the cause of reconciliation and peace. The books published reflect the views of their authors and do not represent the official position of the Maryknoll Society. To learn more about Maryknoll and Orbis Books, please visit our website at www.maryknollsociety.org.

Published by Orbis Books, Maryknoll, New York 10545-0308.

Manufactured in the United States of America.

Library of Congress Cataloging-in-Publication Data

Gateley, Edwina.
In God's womb : a spiritual memoir / Edwina Gateley.
p. cm.
ISBN 978-1-57075-847-8
1. Gateley, Edwina. 2. Lay missionaries—Illinois—Chicago—Biography. 3. Lay missionaries—Catholic Church—Biography. 4. Catholics—Illinois—Chicago—Biography. 5. Church work with prostitutes—Illinois—Chicago. 6. Chicago (Ill.)—Church history—20th century. 7. Genesis House (Chicago, Ill.) I. Title.
BX4705.G2588A3 2009
267'.182092—dc22
[B]

2009008668

For all those brave and beautiful women
whom I have met on my journey
and who have been a source of inspiration
and affirmation for me.
May you continue the struggle to fulfill your dreams
and become all you are called to be.

CONTENTS

ACKNOWLEDGMENTS

My deep gratitude goes to Sr. Monique Gautier, CSJ, who walked so closely and so generously with me in the birthing of this book. Without Monique's time, encouragement and amazing computer skills (!) this memoir would not have been possible. Merci beaucoup!

Thanks also go to my perceptive and talented editor, Mike Leach, whose suggestions were sometimes tough to accept but greatly improved the work!

What a team!

INTRODUCTION

One of the questions most frequently asked of me is: "Why are you still a member of the Roman Catholic Church? Why are you still working full time in the Church?" And I can't answer that question in just a few sentences. I can really answer it only through a reflection on my life's experiences. I am here because of my journey, which has brought me to this point after more than forty years of working as a Catholic laywoman in the Church. And so I look back to see where this motivation and passion has come from. It has certainly not come from reading books and studying theology. It has come from my experience of God, something over which I really have not had much control, having only been vulnerable to God's call in my life.

Sitting in Lancaster Cathedral for so many hours during my youth was like being in God's Womb.

CHAPTER ONE

CHILDHOOD

So let me go back to the beginning when, as a very young child, I had my first spiritual experience, which probably set me on the path toward God and led me to an increasing fascination for the Divine.

I was asleep in the same bedroom as my brother in my hometown in England. I was five and he was seven. We were both fast asleep. I woke up in the middle of the night and saw a lady standing at the window looking down at me. She wore a long dress and a veil, and I was fascinated and delighted at the sight of this beautiful shining woman standing in my bedroom!

After looking at her for a little while, I woke my brother, and I remember saying to him, "Look, look, there is a lady who has come to visit us."

When my brother woke up and saw the lovely lady, he immediately began to scream.

My mother rushed up to the room, opened the door, and said, "What's going on? What's happening?"

My brother answered, "There's a ghost, there's a ghost!"

And I said, "There's a lady, there's a lady!"

My mother asked, "What did she look like?"

"She was wearing a long dress," I answered.

My mother paused for a moment and then said, "That was me. I was there, standing at the window." We went back to sleep.

Years later, as I reflected on this event, I knew that my mother had said she was the lady in order to calm us. We all thought we had forgotten about it. But a year or so later my brother and I were transferred to a Catholic school. Because my mother was Protestant we had been going to a Protestant school, but my father, who was a Catholic, returned from the Army and insisted we go to a Catholic elementary school. I remember the first time I walked into the school. I looked around the entrance hall and there was the lady! It was a statue of Mary.

I said to my brother, "Look, look, there she is! That's the lady who came to visit us!"—and then my brother and I knew who the lady was. We had seen the Virgin Mary.

That experience has never left me, and I know it was real. For me it was the beginning, subconsciously, of my call to serve God through the Church. I have never talked or written about the experience before; it has remained a secret between my brother and me. But after we became adults, my brother one day cautiously asked me, "Do you remember seeing that vision of Mary?" (He was obviously checking out whether I had the same memory!) He had not forgotten. We both agreed, in our adulthood, that the shining lady was the Virgin Mary.

My path was set.

There is absolutely no question that I was a devout Catholic. From those early days, once I was introduced to the Church, baptized a Catholic, and then confirmed, the Church became the center of my life. And so throughout my teenage years I would spend whatever time I could in my church, which was the city cathedral.

While other kids were playing games, kicking ball, and goofing around, I would be sitting in this huge old dark mysterious cathedral, absolutely fascinated by the sense of mystery and awe that I found there. It became for me a secret garden, my haven. From the age of twelve I would creep into that cathedral as though I were entering into a great and holy womb. I would be transfixed for hours, sometimes two to three hours at a time. I always felt very privileged to be in

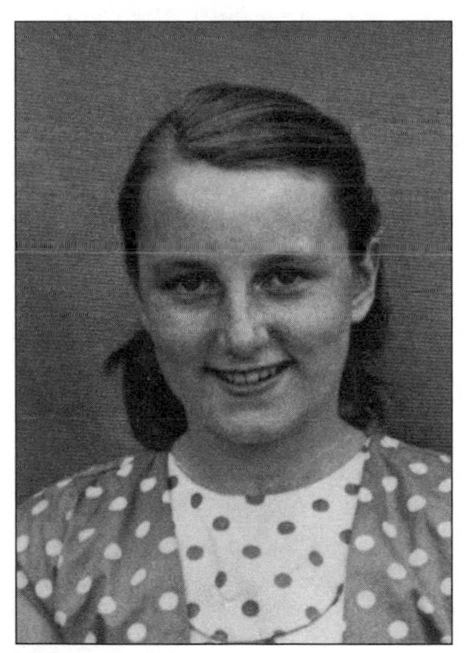

As a girl I went to Mass three times on Sunday and Benediction every Saturday. I almost lived in church, and I loved it.

God's house. Years later I realized that I had started practicing contemplation at the age of thirteen. As a child I experienced being enveloped by God. I really did not have anything to say because I was too stunned by the sense of Presence to say anything, but again it was an experience that left me knowing, without question, that I was called by God. I never doubted that I would say yes, and that, wherever my journey took me, I would be faithful, fundamentally, to this experience of God that was already seeded deep within me. My understanding of God and Church did not come from teachings or from outside of me; it came from inside me, and I think it led me to trust my gut, my instinct and intuitions. Visions and dreams, in which the Christian tradition is steeped, were not at all unusual or odd for me in my young years.

Sitting in the cathedral for so many hours during my youth was like sitting in God's Womb—feeling surrounded and held by God. It was dark in the cathedral and I would always sit near the front, fascinated by all the angel figures and the statues around the altar. Years later I wrote how I felt about that experience:

The Cathedral

It was here, in this great and grey cathedral,
that you surprised and captured me—

a child in school tie and blazer
held awestruck by the vast silence
and cool dampness
of these pillars and frescoed walls,
with gold angels' wings,
set in rows against a thousand stars,
virgins, saints, and martyrs
clasping lilies and jeweled staffs...

And there, hanging before me
by the fourth pew,
the great silent crucifix
bearing down
and breathing upon me
its lonely mystery.
Statues solid and secure,
speaking calm and peace
to my staring eyes
seeking to catch them out
in movement.

Massive sacred altar for the blessed!
How I loved the ritual and the liturgy,
its incomprehensible movements and
    language—
secret cult of which I was a silent part.
And the great grey cathedral
was mine!—

mine in which to wander and be amazed,
mine in which to cry and whisper,
awed by a mighty sense of being.

It was here, in this great grey cathedral
that you surprised and captured me.
It was here,
when I was so young, so naïve,
and so ready to love,
that you stole from your shadows
upon me
and clasped me,
your whisper echoing from the great
stone pillars,
rushing past the rows of angels' wings
and reaching from the sacred altar.
Yes, it was here,
here that you broke through your splendid
fortress
and bent to kiss and claim
an amazed and wondering child.

So it was that the mystery of God captured me many years ago. I devoured every possible piece of literature I could on the saints and the mystics, the martyrs, the virgins and the holy women and men of the Church. We used to have Catholic Truth Society pamphlets on display at the back of the church. I read all of them. I went to Mass three times on Sundays, and Benediction every Saturday. I joined the Sodality of Our Lady and the Legion of Mary. I learned Latin so that I could sing in the choir. I almost lived in church. It was my life. And so very early on in my mid-teens I made a promise that I would give my life to God. How that was to pan out I did not know, but I did know that God was pre-eminent in my life and that I felt called and chosen.

Every morning and every afternoon I would walk along the canal bank back and forth to school. During those walks I maintained an incessant conversation with God—talking to, listening to, and often admonishing the Divine about my schoolwork, my future—whatever. I got so involved with these inner conversations that I was often unconscious of people passing by. Not infrequently I would suddenly catch the bewildered gaze of someone clearly concerned and surprised at seeing this schoolgirl talking to herself with great animation!

God and I had much to discuss, and I was very passionate about it all. I made a child-like bargain with God. If God helped me pass all my school exams (senior high school) with honors, then I would be a missionary in Africa.

I passed all my subjects with honors. In September 1961 I went to Catholic College in Manchester, England, in order to qualify as a teacher and fulfill my promise of becoming a missionary. My commitment never wavered.

CHAPTER TWO

AFRICA

I spent nearly three years in Africa. Living a very simple lifestyle, I ate mostly bananas and peanut stew and carried my own water. There was no electricity in my little mud house. I was responsible for teaching sixty-eight children between the ages of eleven and eighteen, and I had

Fresh out of college and at home in Africa in 1964.

just a handful of books. But I loved the students. I learned the language of the people and participated as fully as I could in the life of the village. Still, I was lonely. As a laywoman, not being a sister or a member of a religious or missionary community, I was very much on my own. The nearest little town was eighteen miles away. As the only white person in the village, I suffered a lot from a sense of isolation and separation from my own culture. Nevertheless, I loved the African people who were teaching me so much more than I could ever teach them.

In Africa my understanding of God changed because of the hospitality, generosity, and openness of the African people. Their notion of God seemed to be so much bigger than what I had learned from my Church at home. But it connected with my experience of God as a child—when I had felt God as all-enveloping, huge, mysterious, and yet very real. I knew that a relationship with God belonged to us all and that it was not just about a Sunday event—going to church, singing and praying for an hour or so with God, and then leaving and getting on with our lives. I learned that we are suffused with God. I came to understand that we walk in God and God gets bigger to the degree that we are open and expectant. It was the African people who introduced me to this notion of God because they embraced me with amazing hospitality. They welcomed me into their homes and constantly gifted me with eggs and chickens, pineapples and fruits. Even though they hardly knew me, they made me feel like I was the most significant person in their lives. The African people demonstrated to me the reality of the gospel mandate to love one another. Hospitality is fundamental to the gospel. The African people surrounded me with gospel hospitality. I was from the West and I was white, foreign, and female. The Africans spoke a different language and I was of a different culture, but we celebrated being together in friendship and hospitality. There was real sisterhood and brotherhood.

God got bigger.

In spite of my love for the Church, as a laywoman I felt that I did not quite fit because I was not a religious sister and there really was no niche for me as a laywoman. One could be a volunteer and that was it. But I did not want to just give a couple of years "helping." God was my life. Mission was my life. The Church was my life. I was totally committed but did not belong on any serious level. It was expected that, after three years of volunteering, one would go home and be "normal." One would have done one's bit for the Church and mis-

I am NOT an elephant.

sion and was now expected to "settle down" and be a normal layperson. But I felt called to be totally involved in the Church's mission as a woman and a layperson, not as an appendage like a volunteer. It was never sufficient for me.

Eventually I succumbed to malaria and became ill a number of times. I knew that I could not continue living in that kind of poverty and isolation, and I was advised to go home, and to try and fit back into life in England. But I never really could—I would never be the same as I had been before going to Africa. My experiences in Africa affected me deeply and permanently, as the following excerpt from my journal of that time clearly shows:

April 17, 1965

Ann Marie was nine years old and sat with all the gracefulness of a Muganda child on the woven palm mat. She looked up at me with her great, brown eyes and flashed a gleaming smile of white teeth. I was her friend—her best and only white friend. She clung to my company like a limpet and I to her as if she were a little shadow, indispensable. The child came from a nearby small mud hut where she lived with her aged grandmother who was severely paralyzed. Ann Marie looked after her grandmother and supported both of them by working in the banana plantations most of her time.

Today was Sunday. It was a special day because no one worked on Sunday and we were going on a trip.

Ann Marie jumped up and down excitedly, her eyes dancing. Even her tight, shining curls seemed to be bouncing with joy.

"Tugenda?" she whispered.

"Yes, Ann Marie, we are going now," I replied in the same African language. We could have been going to lots of beautiful places that hot Sunday afternoon; I almost felt as if I were back in England taking my younger sister to the seaside. Instead, here I was setting out with my little African friend to visit a hidden and distant leper camp in the African bush.

Ann Marie scrambled into the car and soon the wheels were whipping up clouds of dust as we drove along the narrow, dusty road. The almost white sun blazed in the vast blue sky and I felt the heat prickling through my skin. My little charge had quieted down by this time and sat looking back at the disappearing banana trees and the grass huts as we left them behind in the dust.

The noise of the engine attracted numbers of naked or scantily clad black children who peered from the bush and jumped and waved wildly, "*Muzungu! Muzungu!*" meaning "White person! White person!"

The cries of the African children and Ann Marie's triumphant, shrill responses echoed in my ears. It seemed strange to think that only a few months ago I had been sitting for my finals in an English college. A student's life, exams, parties, and dances all seemed so remote now as we bumped along through the green and hot splendor of the East African bush.

The thick yell of a laughing bird startled me and I felt a pulse of fear or maybe nervous anticipation as we neared our destination. I had never visited a leper camp before and I was slightly apprehensive, not being sure of what kind of welcome a young European woman such as myself would receive. I felt grateful for the company of Ann Marie.

The tattered sign read: "Leper Camp—3 miles," and pointed to an almost imperceptible branch off from the dusty road along which we were traveling. The path eventually disappeared altogether and left us following a rough line of clearing through the leafy bush. Monkeys swung and chattered above our heads, swooping audaciously from one palm twine to another. I was amazed at their speed and agility.

"*Eri! Eri!*" cried Ann Marie pointing to a small clearing on the left. There, standing almost in a circle, were low mud huts with corrugated iron or grass roofs and squat holes for windows. At first glance the settlement seemed to be pervaded by an atmosphere of quiet and loneliness—or was it the air of silent suffering that sent a wave of fear through my heart? As soon as the noise of the engine had faded to silence, Africans young and old appeared from every side, congregated in small groups, stopped, stood and stared at the white intruder.

For a moment I felt completely afraid and alien before the strong and cautious gaze of hundreds of pairs of black eyes. I tried not to look at the terrible signs of leprosy that gnawed at the skinny bodies. Instead, I felt a deep compassion rising from within me as I held out both my hands to the headman of the camp. He offered the same greeting and I clasped his ten finger butts. The atmosphere of suspicion broke, and delight flooded the diseased and broken faces.

Mothers, young and old, sat on grass verges outside the huts and cradled in their arms black bundles of wide-eyed, frothy-haired babies. Children clustered round their elders, clutching at the ragged tatters of clothing that hung limply from the leprous bodies. Poor kids, I thought. How very different they were from the children at home in England. The children here had no education; toys were unheard of; pretty—or even decent—clothes were non-existent; birthdays, parties, the joys of Christmas, and outings were totally unknown in this isolated and alienated community.

In their own language the adults thanked me for coming to visit them: "Thank you, thank you, for coming to see us!" They asked for nothing, but their joy was intense at welcoming a white visitor. Followed by crowds of people, the headman showed me around the camp. I saw the squat grass huts used as kitchens and storerooms, and the primitive sanitation—merely six-foot-deep holes enclosed by narrow grass walls. The huts where the people lived were simple one-roomed shelters, dark and dull with a couple of old chairs and maybe a small table, or no furniture at all. The people sat and ate on grass mats, which they wove themselves. They lived on boiled hard bananas that grew in abundance all around and which, when prepared, had a consistency similar to that of our mashed potatoes.

The lepers stared at me as I looked around. They gazed in awe at the shoes I wore—symbols of wealth and privilege. The children were fascinated by my soft fair hair and scrambled round to touch and grasp my white hands. At the entrance of one of the mud huts, an old man leaning on a stick followed my every movement with his narrow dark eyes; both his legs were about a foot in circumference, the skin cracked and scabbed with leprosy. Those whose faces the disease had attacked were pitiful pictures of humanity defaced with mountainous lumps of flesh. My heart went out to all these outcast people and I felt a creeping sense of shame and guilt at what, in comparison, I can only call my life of luxury in England.

The headman invited Ann Marie and me to eat with his family in their mud hut and I readily accepted the invitation—knowing that to refuse would be discourteous. We sat on palm mats in a circle around a large dish of boiled bananas and helped ourselves, using small pieces of strong leaf instead of spoons or forks; we also ate cassava—a sticky, white substance that at other times I had used as glue or chalk. The tea, which we drank from old cups, bottles, and glasses, was a grayish color and had an obscure and unidentifiable taste. It was a meal that I knew I would never forget. Sitting cross-legged among the happy lepers who had never eaten with a white woman before, I had one of my first experiences of a different, but so very real—Eucharist. The downbeats of celebration sounded throughout the bush, and the children danced in a circle while the adults clapped and smiled joyfully. This little "concert" was a token of their gratitude for my visit. The beating drums and the shrill voices of the children moved me more profoundly than any music I had ever heard before. This music had a peculiar, primitive beauty of its own. I smiled and thought of the Beatles.

An hour later I was saying goodbye to my new African friends. As I bent to take the hands of the grubby, smiling children, I felt I wanted to do so much to bring some joy and pleasure into their lives. But the lepers made me feel as if I had given them a fortune. They stood in their tattered, meager clothing and their eyes shone with a happiness that touched me deeply. I had given them something that had cost me nothing, merely a short visit; if I had given them an abundance of food, money, or clothing, I do not think their delight would have been any greater.

They were grateful in the deepest sense of the word and, as I turned and waved goodbye, I felt that here, in this primitive and stricken camp, I had experienced true love and true delight. I had experienced God.

As the car bumped away into the bush and the sight of the many black hands waving receded, I held back tears and silently said to myself the words of the writer, Robert Louis Stevenson: "I blessed God that I was free to wander, free to hope, and free to love."

It was hard to leave behind a people who had received me with such generosity, kindness, and love. But it was time for me to go. Perhaps I had learned all that I needed to know at that point.

CHAPTER THREE

THE VOLUNTEER MISSIONARY MOVEMENT

Back in England, settling down would mean getting an apartment, a job, a boyfriend, and going to church on Sundays. This is what would be normal! I tried it. I did all those things, but my sense of being called, of doing something more fulfilling, never left me, and I knew that praying, paying, and obeying would never be enough for me. I had fallen in love with a God who was too big to be contained within such a small world. There had to be more. There had to be other ordinary men and women who, like me, also felt called to mission.

I had seen the poverty in Africa, the enormous need for education, health care, sanitation, agricultural and technical training, and every aspect of development. A lack of basic education and health care contributed enormously to poverty. Jesus said, "I have come that they may have life, and have it to the full" (John 10:10). There was no shortage of educated people at home in England. They had been privileged with skills and education—as I myself had. To me, the gospel call was clear: we were to share our gifts and talents with the poor. But not only that—we were to share the Spirit of Christ, the Spirit of love, charity, and friendship. I saw mission not as preaching or converting but as a cyclical process of giving and receiving, mutual learning and growing. I knew that in Africa I had received far more than I had been able to give. My vision and understanding of gospel and community had been broadened by the spontaneity, openness, generosity, and hospitality of the African people with whom I worked and lived. This was something to bring back and share with our somewhat more sedate and controlled Church at home.

I was inspired—no, driven—to share my vision of mission and to seek a way to involve others who would respond to the needs that I had seen, as well as to deepen their own experience of Church.

The Vatican Council documents had been published in the mid-sixties and reading them affirmed my belief that lay people are called to be fully involved in Church and mission. I gave up my teaching job and my apartment and set out to find support to start a lay missionary movement. This was a difficult time because of resistance from the Church hierarchy to the new idea of lay people taking responsibility to be Church. An interview with the then cardinal archbishop of Westminster, John Carmel Heenan, resulted in his pronouncement to me: "I give you no authority to found such a movement in the Church at this time. The time is premature." So much for the Vatican Council documents! I was utterly deflated. But the dream was not.

Eventually, after eighteen months of searching and talking to as many bishops and religious leaders as would listen, my vision became a reality. The Volunteer Missionary Movement (VMM) was founded in April 1969 in London. I was alone in a three-bedroom house that had been provided for the new venture by the Missionary Societies of England and Wales. I prayed that God would bless the dream! I got a cat! I got a telephone! I got a typewriter! I started advertising—and people came! Men and women wrote to me from all parts of England, Canada, the United States, and Europe, stating they wanted to be missionaries! Mission, indeed, was not just for priests and religious! The Catholic Church had not yet tapped into the gifts of the laity. We had been shortchanging God. I knew that we diminished our potential as Church when we failed to recognize and claim that all of us are called to be disciples—and even saints and mystics.

As more and more lay people came forward to offer their services as teachers, nurses, builders, plumbers, and a host of other professions, we needed a much bigger place to gather and have our own orientation and training program. I remember meeting with a small group of our lay missionaries to discuss finding a house that could be used as a center. We prayed and we prayed, "Please God, send us a house for our new lay missionary movement." Weeks went by and months went by. Nothing happened. And then I began to think that if we *really* believed and trusted that God was with us, why were we concerned, and why did we worry about this, and why didn't we just thank God for the gift of the house, knowing that all had already been given in faithfulness?

We used to have a prayer group that met every Tuesday night at my house. Some of the seminarians from the nearby seminary would come and join us. We would sit in a circle and pray for an hour. I remember praying aloud at one point and saying, "Thank you, God, for the house you have given to us with thirty rooms and a few acres of land. We're very grateful for this!"

At the end of the prayer gathering, the seminarians came up and said, "That's wonderful! Where is the house?" And I said, "Well, you know, that's the only problem! I don't know *where* it is. But we're giving thanks for the house that God has already chosen!" The guys looked at me as if I was mad.

Not long after that, a friend called me and said, "You know, there is a house only a few miles from here that's quite substantial. It's got thirty rooms and four acres of land."

"That's it!" I declared. "That's ours! We've found it! Who does it belong to?"

My friend answered, "It's a diocesan property. I guess it belongs to the cardinal."

I called the cardinal's office and I ended up talking to the vicar general who invited me to come to London and talk with him. I went and met with the vicar general in his office. I was rather impressed that he had a glass of sherry waiting for me and he treated me with great respect as someone rather important!

His first question was, "Do you wish to buy or rent?"

I just looked at him. "What?" I exclaimed.

The vicar general then said, "Well, the rent is $1,000 a month."

I said, "I can't do that!"

He looked at me and said, "What about $750?"

I said, "I can't do that either!"

He said, "How much *have* you got?"

I said, "I don't have *any* money!"

He looked at me as if he could not believe it. "You have *nothing*?!"

I said, "That's right, but this is the house God has given to us for our lay missionary work."

The vicar general nearly fell off his chair! Then I told him the story of how we had been praying and how God would give what we needed, and that when I heard about the size of this house I knew it was perfect and I never questioned the fact that it would be a direct gift.

The vicar general stood up, looked at me, and said, "I need to leave you for a moment," and he stepped out of the room. Apparently he went to see the cardinal (Basil Hume) in the next office. He came back about fifteen minutes later and said, "Edwina, the house is yours, for $2 a year. And you can have it on a fifteen-year lease."

God is faithful.

And so I ended up with this empty house outside London, with thirty rooms and four acres of land. The house had been used by the diocese in the past as a youth center.

"Edwina," Cardinal Hume said, "this house is yours for two dollars a year!"

So I went to see it and it was then that I realized the problem . . . the repairs that were needed—and, worst of all, the fire regulations! The fire department came. We were ready to move in. I had twenty-three missionaries ready to attend the orientation program.

But the fire department said, "No, you can't have people living here until you upgrade the facility so it is in compliance with the fire regulations."

I said, "How much is that going to cost?"

The estimate came in at approximately $20,000. I did not have any money. But I knew there was a Catholic foundation in London that gave grants. So I made an appointment to see the director of this foundation. It was October. I visited him in his office in London. I told him I needed $20,000. He replied that he would give me an application form to submit to the board at their meeting next year.

"But I need it now!" I exclaimed. "Because of fire regulations we can't move in!"

He looked at me as if he were talking to someone not of sound mind and said, "Edwina, when you apply for a grant it takes a minimum of six months and we have to consider it seriously. You can't just walk in here and ask for $20,000!"

I said, "But we *really* need it now. This is the house God has given us."

He looked at me in disbelief, but he gave me the form and I left. Very quickly I sent the application back with a cover letter emphasizing that we needed the money urgently. On Christmas Eve, which was two months later, I got a telephone call from him, saying, "I wanted you to have a good Christmas. There is a check in the mail for $20,000 for the fire regulation upgrades."

So I look at happenings like this and I know that God listens, and if we truly believe and expect miracles with an indignant faith, God responds. The problem is that such expectancy often leaves us looking a little foolish!

Very soon after moving into the big house I began to feel the need for a place to withdraw and be apart, to be alone and pray. In the overgrown orchard of the property there was an old shed that had once been used for storing tools. It was a bit of a run-down place, but immediately on seeing it in the woods I thought, "Ah! This could be a place to be alone and pray."

I cleaned it out and put in a cot, a little desk, and a chair. The tool shed was the place to which I would, from time to time, withdraw in order to be alone with God and stay in touch with the silence that helped me recognize the presence of God. At one point, I stayed there for a full week and wrote the *Spirit and Lifestyle of the Volunteer Missionary Movement*. That was more than forty years ago. And the *Spirit and Lifestyle of the* VMM became the heart, the charism of the Movement. Today it is still prayed and studied and used as a guide and inspiration for the VMM. Even though it was written so long ago, I myself am amazed that it still speaks today to our contemporary lay missioners:

The spirit and calling
Of the VMM missionary is,
First and foremost,
One of love and service
In and to the world.
As laypeople we give a
Special witness
To the reality that all
The People of God
Are called to involvement.
In Christ's mission
All are called to serve.
Bishops, builders, and nurses alike
Must work together
Equally
Towards the coming of the Realm of God.
Mission is given
To us all.

The VMM grew. This new and exciting lay movement took root and expanded until there were over five hundred of us—male and female, young and old, married and single—working in twenty-six different countries on five continents. The Movement flourished—and so did I! Or so I thought, because I became rather famous I suppose. I was now friend of bishops and the then cardinal of England and Wales—Basil Hume. My picture appeared in the Catholic

The first group of VMM missionaries. In less than ten years we had recruited, prepared, and sent more than five hundred missioners overseas. We were the fastest growing and largest lay missionary movement in the world.

newspaper! I was on a roll, so to speak. I felt fulfilled. The calling had been realized—my dream had come true. God was faithful.

But I began to feel a stirring within me. It was like the feeling I had when I was first called to Africa, and the one I had when I was called to start the VMM. There was something inside me urging me to move in a new direction—even though I felt quite happy where I was. I was doing very well. I was settled. I was successful and seemingly content.

But I could not deny the insistence of this inner call. I was being invited to let go. But I did not want to. I was settled. My mission was in full swing! In less than ten years we had recruited, prepared, and sent hundreds of lay missioners overseas. We were the fastest growing and largest lay missionary movement in the Western world. We were builders, farmers, accountants, doctors, teachers, nurses, engineers, veterinary surgeons, administrators, and technicians. We were vibrant and alive and we represented a whole new vision of mission in the Catholic Church. Eventually, though not without protest from some Catholic bishops, we became ecumenical. Yes—the VMM was definitely a new young thing! But, as a consequence of calling forth a new spirituality and, in particular, becoming ecumenical, we lost our funding from the bishops of England and Wales. It was a hard blow.

We began to preach in churches in order to raise our own funds for our many missions; we opened offices in Scotland, in Ireland, and, eventually, in the United States. The VMM was a breath of fresh air in the Catholic Church and very much a child of Vatican II.

I had found my mission and I loved it! But there was no denying another call that I felt stirring deep within me. This disturbed me—particularly when everything was going so well and I felt a tremendous sense of fulfillment. How could I let go of everything that had given me a sense of identity and belonging? How could I start again? In spite of such questions, however, I knew at a deep level that it was time to go. Is God ever satisfied? No. God is a great seducer—ever inviting us deeper into the journey.

Letting go of the VMM would be one of the hardest things I had ever done. I had founded it and run it for ten years. But I knew I needed to take time out to ponder what I was feeling inside. Deep down, I think, I was hoping that God would be satisfied if I went on retreat and spent some quality time in prayer. God would then leave me in peace to continue being the director and president of the VMM, to enjoy all the satisfaction and accolades that came with the position. I had been very busy and preoccupied with work and traveling, and I knew that I really did need to put aside some time for God. I needed to listen.

CHAPTER FOUR

THE SAHARA DESERT

I went to the Sahara desert in Algeria, North Africa, and stayed for three months. I would never be the same again.

The Sahara desert is hundreds and hundreds of miles of nothing—of sand just stretching far, far away and disappearing into the sky. There are also volcanic areas of large boulders and rocks that have stood in the same place for thousands of years. Lizards dart everywhere. There are tarantulas that hide under rocks. The cockroaches are about five inches in length. The silence is total. I have never experienced such a silence, ever, in my life.

My retreat in the Sahara was truly "down-time" with God. There was no one for me to talk to, there was no activity for me to be involved in, there was simply nothing to do! I was alone with myself and God. On reflection, it was a time of sinking into a consciousness of the Divine. I was extremely privileged and blessed to have this opportunity, in spite of the total loneliness, the solitude, and the simplicity of my lifestyle. It was a very rich and deep experience, one that increased my sense of belonging to God and being deeply loved.

The awareness of this love gave me an inner confidence to trust my intuitions and sense of God's presence. I did not know it then, but my time in the desert would lead me to such a consciousness of God's all-embracing presence and inclusive love that I would, in the future, be impelled to question and challenge the control and limitations of my Church.

I came to know, with a great certainty, that God longs to comfort us and to assure us that, no matter what we have done, where we have been, or even how we have lived—we will never be abandoned or excluded from God's embrace. Perhaps the best way to share these convictions is to dare (and not without some trepidation) to offer some extracts from the journal I wrote at the time.

Excerpts from the Desert

June 7, 1979

This land is amazing. What place could compare with this? The sands stretch out everywhere—brown and yellow and bleached. The territory is inhospitable, full of rocks, crater-like formations, needle and dome-shaped mountains thrusting up to dramatically break the flatness around. Part of it reminds me of the moonscape I saw on TV—but that was a little screen. This is vast and I feel so tiny, so tiny before its magnificence. And the silence—yes, that is part of this desert drama. The utter solitude is almost frightening, awesome in its magnitude. For many, many miles there is not a soul around except perhaps for a solitary nomad watching his goats. I have never felt so physically and utterly alone.

I set off at 7:30 in the morning. The wind howled through the mountains. I felt suddenly desolate and isolated as I struggled along the mountain path carrying a few books and a flask of water. I was like a mad pilgrim, a crazy hermit determined to wander in the wilderness. The mountain was not difficult to climb. At the top I found a secluded ledge, a fine place to sit and gaze at the incredible scenery of the Sahara far into the horizon. Prayer is inevitable amidst such grandeur. And my heart was full of it, full of praise to God for all creation. One becomes very much aware of how small one is in the immensity of the desert. Here one hardly dares speak, doesn't want to speak. Here one is silenced.

In the desert, also, the Old Testament comes alive. The rugged scenery, the wandering nomads with their goats, and the shimmering heat. I imagine Abraham with his flock, the prophets in the wilderness, and the journeying of the people of Israel through the desert. I simply watch, imagine, and am filled with quiet joy. As the sun rises higher, the heat intensifies and I climb down the mountain. I walk across the wide and stony plateau until I can look down into a vast sandy valley where goats graze around a nomad. Moving to the edge of the cliff I find another rocky ledge and here I stay, praising God until the sun has set behind the hills. Alleluia!

June 8, 1979

As I sat in the solitude of the desert to pray, I heard these words and and wrote them down:

Go in my Name
and I shall be your staff
and I shall be your buckler
and your helmet and your shield.
And your words will be filled
with my wisdom,
your eyes will shine with my beauty
and your skin will be fresh
as the dawn,
and I shall be in your heart.
The steps you take
will be my steps,
and your sandals will be mine.

I will fill your bag
and be your staff.
There will be a great shadow
of anguish and of darkness
and it shall pass over you
as a cloud,
hanging heavy and oppressive.
But I shall be there
and my light will rise up
to dispel the shadow of anguish,
for mine are your sandals
and I am your staff
and I shall fill your bag.
You shall know joy in my path
and my Spirit will breathe in you
for you are my prophet,
my priestess,
my servant,
and I am
your God.

And my soul responded:

I will be your prophet,
and you shall be my staff,
and you shall fill my bag,
for I am your servant,
and you are my God.

And I prayed aloud on the mountain:

Hear me!
God of Abraham, Isaac, and Jacob,
hear the voice of your servant,
for I call to you in the wilderness,
I claim you as my God
and I am your servant.
And I cry, O God,
that I might serve you
as Abraham, as Isaac, as Jacob,
as Peter and Paul,
as all of them
who went before.
And I am a woman, God,
and I speak with the voice of a woman
And I love with a woman's heart.
And I am your servant, God,
your daughter.
And I call, God,
that I might be your prophet.
Look upon your daughter
and hear my voice,
the voice of a woman,
the voice, O God,
that cannot be stilled
in the proclamation of your Name.

And it will ring loud and clear
on the mountains, on the hilltops,
and on the rooftops.
The voice, O God,
will be your Voice
And I, the woman,
will be your prophet,
your daughter.

June 10, 1979

I went up into the mountain
to watch with God.
I was afraid,
for although the moon shone
over all the land,
there were shadows in the hills
and I feared them.
The rocks slid beneath my feet—
poorly shod—
till I found a place
sheltered by two huge boulders
on either side.
I crouched and sat
in the rocky crevice,
and I watched the moon above,
white and splendid,

mastering the clear sky.
O God, your servant is here!
And all was silent in the darkness
and I was tiny
before the vast emptiness.
O God, I am here—
to watch with you.
The silence was mighty
and I was afraid.
I felt the wings of a creature
brush against my hair
and the flutter
of its body.
I am terrified!
O God, you must speak to your servant!
I took the Bible and opened it:

"How I love your place
    Yahweh Sabaoth!
How my soul yearns and pines
    for Yahweh's courts!
My heart and my flesh sing for joy
    to the living God.

"The sparrow has found its home at last,
    the swallow a nest for its young,
Your altars Yahweh Sabaoth,
    my Lord and my God.

"Happy those who live in your house
and can praise you all day long;
And happy the pilgrim inspired by you
with courage to make the Ascents.

"As they go through the Valley of the Weeper,
they make it a place of springs,
Clothed in blessings by early rains,
Thence they make their way from height to height
soon to be seen before God on Zion..."
(Psalm 84)

When I read this psalm by the light of my flashlight, my heart leapt up for joy, for God had listened and heard me, and through the psalm, God spoke to me. Then the long hours of the night from the moon rising and falling to the dawn creeping up passed in joy and praise—for God was with me, and together we watched, and together we sat in the shadows of the mountain.

"With his pinions he will cover you,
and under his wings you shall take refuge;
his faithfulness is a buckler and a shield.
You shall not fear the terror of the night
nor the pestilence that roams in darkness
nor the arrow that flies by day.

No evil shall befall you,
Nor shall affliction come near your tent..."
(Psalm 91)

I had no doubt that God was speaking directly to me on the mountain. The strength of God was with me, gentle and compassionate. I feared not the terror of the night, but I watched with love and praise the coming and the glory of the dawn.

June 13, 1979

Now my God, my friend, I am here in the desert. I have come here to You as I came to You in the silence of the cathedral as a child. I come again to be alone with You, to share with You, to listen and to watch with You. Our covenant stands. I am your servant and You are my God. What would You have me do? I have no life without You and do not exist without You. With the same enthusiasm, desire, and longing I had as a child I come again and say:

Here I am.

June 15, 1979

"The Spirit of Yahweh has been given to me
For Yahweh has anointed me." (Isaiah 61)

The Old Testament is full of stories telling of God's direct intervention in people's lives. The prophets are called and God speaks to them clearly, making the message known. Why, indeed, should we not believe that God speaks to us as clearly and directly today? I believe God's voice comes to us in our own day as it did in the past. And those who have ears to hear will hear. I believe we are usually deaf to God's voice.

> "These people have ears but do not hear, eyes
> but do not see...
> for the heart of these people is grown dull..."
> (Jeremiah 5:21, 23)

I know that God has called me and anointed me as God did the prophets, the apostles, and many men and women since. But such a call is something we do not talk about. We are afraid of visions and dreams, even though much of our faith tradition is based so much on them! How is it that we believe in all the stories and revelations of the past but do not trust the revelations and the voice of God in the present? Is it that we do not believe that God speaks today? Are we deaf to God's voice? Are we afraid of being ridiculed? Dismissed? Maybe considered a little mad?

But I must write about such things, for they have come to me in deep prayer. I know that God sends me wherever God wills—to the ends of the earth, to the wilderness, to the city. And God's Spirit is upon me and God's words are in my mouth. It is only for me to be totally available. I am here for God and I cannot doubt this calling. I know I am to share God's love and it is this love that most amazes me—how God longs for each and every one of us that we might know how much we are loved. God will use me as a channel of this love. I am filled with joy and humbled to be so called and even more amazed to understand how God's plans stretch far beyond our time span.

> "Before I formed you in the womb, I knew you.
> Before you came to birth I consecrated you."
> (Jeremiah 1:5)

These lines remind me of the conviction I had as a child that God was very present in my life and had a plan for me. It never fails to amaze me how God is so faithful, even when we are not. God is forever there, forever waiting, forever longing for us to come home.

> "But Yahweh is waiting to be gracious to you
> To rise and take pity on you." (Isaiah 30:18)

God never gives up but waits for us, forever, to turn back and remember God's love. This has happened to me many times, and I have always known that God would be waiting for me. The knowledge doesn't stop us from failing; it only makes us more aware of God's tremendous love. I have much to be thankful for. God loves me in spite of all my failings. Who am I, and what am I, that God should choose to use me, to have need of me and to work God's miracles through me? Of course I am amazed and I believe, I believe so much in this great love. I can think of no greater joy, no greater privilege, than to spend my life loving and serving this incredible God of ours. May God use me to the full.

In Solitude

There is a peace here which surely must
    be rare,
For it is very deep—it soaks into the bones.
It steals in with the moon-filled night
And envelops this tiny stone hut—
Gently, silently.
Peace. All sleeps. Enshrouded.
Listen—listen! Silence sleeps.
Even the cockroach crouches unmoving
And the flame in the oil lamp
Is still—
Still.
My spirit stirs with wonder
As God slips—
Almighty Presence—

Into the domain of solitude
And deeply, deeply enters
Every crevice and corner.
Gently, imperceptibly
Holds my soul suspended
In God's mighty silence.

June 23, 1979

One really has to make an effort to do anything here. I am frequently covered in sweat to which the hot,

My hermitage in the Sahara. In the desert the Old Testament came alive.

blowing, and fine sand sticks. Then these huge flies crawl all over me. I must be unrecognizable! But I am alone with God who knows me. It seems I have been alone with God for a long time! But God waits in silence. There is no need to be anxious, for with God there is never any hurry. Now God just watches, looks upon me, and prepares my heart for the work to be done. I do not know the work. I only know I wish with a deep longing to be totally available without reserve and without question. I cannot think of any greater joy than to give myself absolutely to this amazing Lover. Nothing else will satisfy me. Nothing else is enough. This giving must be absolute.

God, hear your servant,
listen to my voice,
for you know me, you know my heart.
You know I thirst, you know I hunger,
and you know, O God, that only you
can fill that hunger.
I will go to the highest mountain,
I will go to the deepest valley,
I will go to the heart of the desert,
I will go to the center of the city,
I will go, O God, anywhere
in your world,
wherever you will send me.
I wait only to hear your voice,

to follow your way,
and to do so in complete abandonment
to your will.
For you are my God and I am your servant.

I am very happy. There is no happiness that can be compared with that of being with God. God supports me and reminds me of his presence. Here I could be a real prey to loneliness and a sense of isolation and insecurity. When I begin to feel lonely, I call upon God to hold me up, and God has never failed me. God is like a father or a mother walking gently behind the child—allowing the child freedom to walk, explore, and wander—but never leaving her shadow and continually attentive in case she should call and reach out her hand.

Surely this God of ours is great in love! How could I be afraid? God is unable to leave me alone. God is my strength, my inspiration, my hope, and all my joy. Do not ask yourself if you have time to pray, ask yourself if you have time to love. For that is what it is.

June 28, 1979

I am spending many hours just sitting with God—even throughout the night. There is no sound, no disturbance, just a gentle silence that invites prayer and union with God in solitude. Again I have this tremendous awareness of being blessed; I feel very strongly that God's love has chosen this place for me—has allowed me to come here specifically to be alone in a place where God knew I could respond and be at peace. I am so grateful for this.

God must have known how I would love it here, how my soul would rejoice and how my spirit would exult! God must have known that here I could only praise and, like a child, bubble over with joy. And so I do. And so, God, you have truly blessed me and filled me. My cup is overflowing. You wanted to show me your love. I have asked to see your wisdom and your wonders. And I see them in abundance.

These wonders were manifest for me in particular when I realized with horror that my water supply, which was stored in a large tin drum sunk in the earth, was inexplicably going down—faster than I was using it! Suddenly I became aware that there was a hairline crack running down the the length of the tank. What would I do without water? How could I survive? After some anxious pondering I decided that I had to take some kind of action—nothing would be achieved by my sitting in the hermitage trembling! So I gathered my courage, took my large water bottle and, noting the position of the sun for direction, I set out into the desert looking for water!

It was a pure act of faith, grounded solely in dependence on divine providence. I walked and walked in the hot sun. The farther I went, the more anxious I grew. How could I possibly find water in this dry wilderness? After about an hour I saw ahead of me what looked to be a pile of stones with a goatskin rug covering them. I squinted in the sunlight and my heart leapt as I detected movement beneath the pile of stones. A woman's head emerged and then she stood tall against the vast sky. She was an Arab Touareg woman, clothed in a long black dress and veil, her face burnt brown by the sun. She saw me and began to walk toward me. But—starved for the presence of another human being—I began to run toward her! As we came close to one another we both stood and stared, amazed at the sight of each other! Well, she belonged there, she was part of the desert scene, but I must have appeared to her as someone from another planet! I could not understand the words she spoke to me in the Touareg tongue, but she held out her hand to me and led me to her hovel of stones. I do not know why she was living alone in the middle of the desert. Maybe she had been evicted from her tribe... maybe she had a disease... maybe she was a prostitute... but she was real and alive and a woman! She bent down to reach into her hut and pulled out a beautifully woven rug, which she placed on the sand. After indicating that I should sit on the rug, she left me and went off toward the volcanic rocks that rose up behind the hut.

For twenty minutes or more I sat alone, wondering if I had made a great mistake—anything could happen to me! But she returned carrying two earthenware mugs and a kettle filled with hot sweet Arabian tea. She poured the tea into a mug and handed it to me. She also gave me goat cheese and olives to eat. It was a feast! We sat in silence, just looking at one another in amazement. We could not communicate verbally, but we did communicate on a much deeper level—two women, one from the East and one from the West, one brown and one white, brought together in the middle of the wilderness to drink tea and feast.

It was Eucharist.

God had provided in great abundance. When the tea was finished, the woman rose and took me again by the hand, leading me to the volcanic boulders. And there, between two great boulders, she pointed to a deep crevice filled with water! God had provided! She filled my bottle, we embraced, and I set off back to my hermitage. I had seen God's Wisdom and the wonder of God's ways.

July 12, 1979

We rarely realize that God takes us seriously. When we pray, ask for things, declare our love, or commit ourselves to God (perhaps in a moment of enthusiasm) God hears and remembers. Somewhere along the line, our prayer of long ago will be answered. For God is faithful and God is watchful. If we were to take

God as seriously as God takes us, the world would be transformed. Let us never imagine, then, that our words and our prayers go unheard. We have no idea with what great love and attention they are listened to by the One who has counted every hair on our heads.

Now when I think in wonder of the ways in which God uses me, when I consider in amazement the fact that God will continue to use me, I remember how, many years ago when I was only a child, with great enthusiasm and zeal I offered my life to God. The memory is so vivid to me that I can at this moment relive the intensity of my confidence and fearlessness before the call of God. I was totally taken up with this beautiful alliance, this covenant, sealed with joy and love between myself and God. And now, older and more mature, I can look back and see with amazement how seriously God took me. So when we pray, let us remember, that every word, every whisper is heard and considered by our great and amazing God.

God takes us seriously. Alleluia!

July 18, 1979 — 10 PM to 5 AM

It is night. I experience a paralysis. I am lying on the mud floor in prayer. There is light everywhere even though it is night. I am deeply conscious of the words I hear:

I am with you. I have always been with you. Before you were conceived I was with you. Be steadfast. Do not be afraid. For I am with you. For I am your staff, I fill your bag, mine are your sandals. My Spirit is in you and I go before you. Do not be afraid, for I shall never leave you. My light will shine upon you, my words will be in your mouth and my wisdom in your heart. Go and be steadfast, I have always been with you.

Where shall you go?

You shall go where I shall lead you and it will be clear to you, for my light is sound and strong and my Spirit will guide you. I have heard your cry in the desert and on the mountaintop. I have been attentive. I am always attentive. And I have blessed you with all the gifts for which you asked—these and others that you do not yet know. These gifts I give to you so that people might know my love. You will be filled that they might be filled. And I shall go before you. And I am your staff, and my Spirit is great in you. Be steadfast. Do not be afraid. For I love you. I have always loved you.

To whom shall you go?

You shall go to my people. Not where you would choose. For I have many servants in Africa and the people of the poor countries know me. I am with them deep in their hearts. They have not rejected me. It is those who do not know me and my love for them to whom you must go. They are many. They live in dark corners—they can be found in taverns and supermarkets and they walk the streets by night while their hearts sob in the light of day. Among them you will find noise and laughter—and also emptiness. They do not know me. They knew me once, but now no longer. Yet still they hunger and thirst and I, their God, stay awake and wait for them, because they are mine and I love them. For them I have given my Son; for these, my loved and lost ones, my Son took on flesh. I raised him up for these whom I love that they might see my light and live in it and be delivered from darkness. These are my people, my children for whom my heart grieves without ceasing. Go to these my people, for they are mine and they are lost. These are my sheep without a shepherd. Night without a star. They do not read the books of learned men—they have no interest in books on prayer or morals or theology. This is another world to them, couched in a strange and frightening language. Such things are of no use to these children of mine. They will not enter churches, or read books about me. Rather, they will remain far from my house. They will stay in the taverns, the streets, and the train stations. And there they cannot find me, for they do not know where to look, how to see. And you, you are my servant and I have blessed you. Your gifts are many. I have given according to my promise. I have fulfilled my covenant with you, and more. As you have been faithful and steadfast, so have I not forgotten you. My Spirit will remain with you, to give you light and strength. My gifts will be a witness to my love. For it is my love of which you must speak—not my power or glory, not my might and majesty—but only of my love. For that is what I am. I am love. This is of the greatest importance. It was for love that I sent my Son. For love he died, so that for love my people might live. Love—my greatest gift—is much neglected, for the learned men have emphasized my glory and in doing so they have neglected my love. This is why people hunger, why they thirst. And they remain in darkness, afraid and alone.

And you—I have filled you with this love—a hundredfold and more. Go to my lonely people, my rejected ones, my lost ones, my brave ones, the ones who wear the masks, the ones who laugh and dance and drink but in their hearts heave and sob. These are my own for whom I grieve. For whom I long. I have loved you forever. I am with you. I go before you. I will never leave you. For you are mine. And I am your God. I have kept my covenant. I have blessed you and more than blessed you. I have heard your voice. I have answered with more riches than you can imagine. You will see my wonders and glimpse my wisdom. For you have knocked and the door was opened to you, you have asked and you have received. But I am a God beyond your understanding—I give a thousandfold to my own even when they do not see. But you, you have been persistent, though I heard you when you first called out to me. You cannot know how my Spirit will work in you. Already you are on my path and I go before you. My Spirit is within you and all is given to you. Do not be afraid. Be steadfast. For I am with you. I have always been with you. I have heard you and have loved you. And now I send you according to

> your wish. But you are not alone. Speak in my name. Do not be afraid of the light I have given you, of the wonders you will perform. They are mine. And they are more than those already seen in you. It is my love. My gifts in you will speak my love. I have fulfilled my covenant according to my promise.

July 20, 1979

We can never know how and when God will speak. We can only be sure that, if we ask, God will respond at the most unexpected time. God is faithful, watchful and waiting all the time for the opportunity to come into our hearts. It takes us a long time to realize this and to prepare ourselves for this coming. Often we think we are ready, but only God knows the right time. For God is faithful and God's love is great. How can we measure it? How can we assess it? If we really knew it, how could we survive?

I waited. I prayed. It seemed a long time—days, weeks, months. "How long my God, how long?" I knew God was there. God is always there. But often we need more than knowledge. We want awareness and fulfillment. In my love I simply accept the reality of the presence of God. It doesn't matter whether I am filled with joy or feel empty and bored. All that matters is that I love. Still, it is beautiful to hear God's voice, it is beautiful to be "taken over" by God's Spirit, it is surely beautiful to be "lost in God."

I said to God, "How long my God, how long?"

I was tired and I was ready for bed, but I found myself questioning God, complaining a little that I had not felt God's presence or heard God's voice. Oh God, how can we begin to understand you? Your answer then came, unexpected and immediate. I was filled with an overwhelming urge to fall prostrate before you.

"Lord, have mercy on me!"...

I could say nothing else. But suddenly you were so much there—vibrant, alive, a living Presence I could feel in every part of my being. You took over. I no longer, it seems, existed. There was only you—a powerful Presence impossible to describe. You filled me, held me, absorbed me—I was held in a swathe of intense energy.

"Lord, have mercy on me!"...

Oh, God, you have not only heard my voice. In your great love you answered me. In your great love you loved me. Watchful, attentive, compassionate God! And who am I?

"Lord, have mercy on me!"

You held me—suspended, conscious only of an enormous love and a magnificent Presence. Smaller, smaller, smaller I became as this great love filled, expanded, transformed.

"Lord, have mercy on me!"...

Time-less. Invisible. Incalculable. Beyond measure. Aware and not aware. Alive and yet as dead. Blind, seeing nothing, yet having seen all—the Vision Beautiful.

"Lord, have mercy on me!"...

And who am I? And who am I? Before this, in this, through this, I am lost, I am diminished. I am reborn. The splendor, the beauty, is not in sight, in feel or touch. It is in the experience of being lost in and taken over by love. Let go. There is nothing anymore to hold on to. All is gone. God is.

"Lord, have mercy on me!"...

I am captivated. I am absorbed. God is sweeping, all enveloping... caressing... embracing...

"Lord, have mercy on me!"...

How long, my God, how long?

Now.

For I am faithful.

For I am Love.

I have waited for you.

I have never looked away from you—

no, not for a single second.

For it is I who wait,

I who love,

without measure—incalculable.

It is I who hold out

the hand

to raise you up.

It is I who wait
for your hand
to reach out and take mine—
ever outstretched.
Now.
Always.
Always.
Now.
"Lord, have mercy on me!"...

Let Your God Love You

Be silent.
Be still.
Alone.
Empty
Before your God
Say nothing.
Ask nothing.
Be silent.
Be still.
Let your God
Look upon you.
That is all.
God knows.
God understands.
God loves you

With an enormous love,
And only wants
To look upon you
With that love.
Quiet.
Still.
Be.

Let your God—
Love you.

The more one experiences God
The smaller one becomes.

The less one speaks
The more God speaks.

July 31, 1979 — Alger

I have now left my desert solitude to spend my last two weeks in the Trappist monastery here in the mountains. It is beautiful—the mountains stretch behind the monastery and the sun sets beyond them. There are many trees here and it is cool and fresh! There is a big chapel like a barn—simple, old, beautiful—and we have daily Mass there and say the daily Night Office. There is also a tiny chapel. God has brought me here in God's love to a place that gives me great joy and peace.

It is so different from the heat and total silence of the desert.

Let me hear your voice, oh God! Here I will once again glimpse your wisdom and see the wonder of your ways. Here I will be silent before your love; here I will glorify you. Here, Lord, I will love you. You are my God and I am your servant. I praise you for leading me with such care and love into the wilderness.

Here in this monastery I hear the sounds of people's voices echoing through the mountains; donkeys bray—they are laden with water panniers from the monastery's water tank. With the coming of night, the people sing and rejoice, for it is Ramadan and now they may eat and drink. There is life all around. And here in this place—blessed with so many years of prayer and toil—God is praised continually. The prayer rises from this small community of monks whose voices praise God day and night. Yes, this is a beautiful place and it is good to be here. I am always amazed by how good God is to me, giving me the best of wine and feeding me with all good things.

August 3, 1979

This time, this precious time, is God's. People ask if I get bored, and the question startles me. I have never even thought of being bored. God is all-absorbing. The hours pass quickly in God's presence. We are simply together and there is a great peace. I want nothing more. Anything else would be a distraction. I only want to be with God. In the silence I listen to God's voice and when I do not hear anything I am joyful and at peace simply in God's presence. It is like a vacation with God—a vacation of quiet love, joy, and peace. It is a vacation where I experience wholeness and fulfillment. I feel I am rich—for such a vacation is rare.

God called me and said: "I want to be with you. I want to spend time with you."

And everything in me said, "Yes!" and rejoiced at the thought of being silent for so long with God. Surely it is a privilege? Surely it is a joy? And I am filled, my cup is overflowing. All has been given to me—even that which I do not know.

When I first began this three-month pilgrimage, I was exuberant and danced round the mountains praising God aloud; my prayer was enthusiastic and joyful and many were my requests to God that I would be a prophet and a disciple, that God would grant me the gifts to enable me to fulfill God's work for me. Now the exuberance has ebbed, melting away into a great calm sea—deep and gentle and beautiful. Now I want only to say, "I love you!" That is all there is to say, and it fills my days and my nights. Love, only love—all else will follow love, all else is taken care of. And now, while we are so much together, with this rare and precious time set aside like a priceless jewel, all I want to do is gaze upon it—to *be* in the presence of God. All I have to say is, "I love you!" and every moment is precious for God is waiting.

This night I will spend in prayer. It will be my sixth night in prayer. These nights are like a secret rendezvous with a lover. Everything is still and dark and silent. The night is all around me and there is God, alone and waiting in the darkness. I smile and say, "Here I am, God. I've come."

Sometimes it seems as if God is asleep with the rest of the house and I say, "I will not leave, God. Though you are silent and I am empty, yet I will not leave." And then the hours moved slowly—the still, still hours of night stretching endlessly until dawn. And when my body reacts against unnatural sleeplessness and I nod and begin to sink into drowsiness, my spirit awakens me and I say, "Oh no, I will not leave! And no, I will not sleep! For I have come to watch with you, God, though I must watch alone! I want you to know I love you, God, and so I will stay with you!" When dawn comes, I watch the light creeping into the chapel like a silent revelation. And I say, "My God, my God, I watched with you! Now wake up—that I might sleep!"

But at other times the hours have passed swiftly and I have been amazed. God has held me up and embraced me, whispering love. Still, silent nights, rich in love and tenderness! All sleep, life sleeps, but here, with God, I am awake—there is only love—and its hold is total, sweet and deep, deep, deep...

August 4, 1979

At first I was afraid. One hears all sorts of strange noises in the night. I listened more to them than to God... "You shall not fear the terror of the night... I have conquered evil... Why are you afraid? Am I not here?"

And I respond in my heart, "Yes, of course, but... listen... what's that?"

"My grace is sufficient for thee."

"Yes, I know all that—but..."

"Be still, and know that I am God. I have waited for you. Why are you so distracted? Have you not come to be with me?"

"Yes, God! I must not care about strange noises. Anyway, this is the house of God and I am in it!... 'With his pinions He shall cover you.' No I am no longer afraid!"

"I have blessed you, I have blessed you."

"Yes, not just a hundredfold, God, but five hundred-fold. No—not just five hundredfold, a thousand-fold!"

"And you will bear fruit a thousand-fold because you have asked and I have heard, because you have knocked on my door a thousand times and I heard you the first time. I have heard all you asked and I shall give it to you. And I shall give you that which you do not know. I have blessed you and you shall bear fruit. I am a faithful God and I listen to my people. And you—you do not whisper—no, you have shouted from the mountaintop. And surely I have heard! I am the God of Abraham, of Isaac and Jacob. I am your God and I love you with a great love. I have always loved you and I will never leave you. Be steadfast and walk with me. For I go before you and you will need no other light. I am your staff, I have filled your bag and mine are your sandals. Because you have asked, all shall be given to you, because your love is great I will bless you, because you have given yourself to me, I will give all to you."

August 5, 1979

I have found that the days pass very quickly, and as each day ends I say, "Edwina, what did you *do*?" And I *did* nothing. I am simply in the company of God, and it seems, even then, there is not enough time. God is very good to me—I do not know why I should be the recipient of so many blessings. But I have never been so deeply at peace or experienced such prolonged periods of joy.

I am amazed at this newly discovered capacity to pray and this newly discovered love of prayer. I never would have believed that I could just *be* with God for so many hours both day and night. I have discovered that if you ask for an inch, God gives you many miles! I say, "God, I'm tired but let me stay and watch with you for just one hour." But then God takes over—and *how* God takes over! My one-hour stretches in joy throughout the night until the dawn. It is as if God is unable to resist the small love we offer.

I have discovered a mighty love—far greater and far more alive than anything I have ever known before. I have discovered a God who is falling over backward to come to us, who waits for the glimmer of faith that prompts us to call upon God. And then God comes—according to the measure of our faith. But first there must be faith and confidence. Then, ah then, when one knocks, God not only opens the door, but lifts the roof off as well! It is a great, great love. And how little we know of it and how little we really seek it!

But this journey of discovery also has its dark times. One must contend with a power that I experience as evil. Perhaps it walks alongside a person where there is solitude and contemplation: where a soul reaches out for God, the power of evil also reaches out for the soul. The experience is real and physical and frightening. It is a force that attacks in quiet and unexpected moments—in the dark of night when all, except evil, is asleep. The experiences for me have been of a physical suffocation—powerful and real—so real that I cannot even cry out because I feel so tightly grasped. And for a while there is a struggle and I am awake and alert—caught unaware. The other experience is one of being pulled at and torn apart—a power pulling me and tearing at me—I can see it! I have been very afraid of these experiences. I know they are of evil, for when I am able to gather the wit and strength to cry out or even just think, "In the name of Jesus Christ..." there is then a radical sense of change in the room. It is as if a powerful presence has suddenly departed and the whole room, the whole atmosphere, breathes peace. I sense relief, and great waves of soothing peace flood through me. I seem to have passed from death to life. The calm is now utter, total. Peace. Where there is God, must evil be so near? I have never experienced it so closely and intensely before. But then, neither have I experienced God so closely and so intensely before.

God has brought me here to be with him in a special way:

> "I am going to lure her and lead her out into
> the wilderness
> and there I will speak to her heart." (Hosea 2)

And so God does! Three months—gone so fast. With God time does not exist; there is only a consciousness of presence and love. We can spend our lives doing good and perhaps hardly begin to be aware of or understand the reality and closeness of God's love in our lives. Perhaps we must have the courage of the diver who plunges straight into the deep, still waters, not knowing how deep those waters are, or what lies beneath the surface. First come the faith and the confidence and then the discovery and the joy. And this voyage goes on and on, for the waters are deeper than we can ever comprehend. The depths are fathomless.

I feel I have only just begun. Now I see a little—but God's revelation is never complete. God is very gentle with us, knowing that we can grasp only so much. I have prayed for a glimpse of God's wisdom and this has been given to me in the gradual progression of these months in the desert. I believe God planned it with care and love, knowing exactly what I needed and how much I could take at any given time.

And now I must set out to do God's work upon the foundation that God has built in me.

"My soul glorifies the Lord
and my spirit rejoices in God my Savior."

August 9, 1979 — 2 AM

I have been very frightened and fully awake all night. I am conscious of murmurings, a sense of prowling and lurking and crouching.

Oh I was so afraid! In the chapel I said: "God, I am afraid. Why am I afraid when you are with me? Forgive me my human weakness and hold me up." But I did not stay beyond midnight. I was too afraid. I returned to my room.

In the night evil came—as always, under cover of darkness. And I knew it when it came—for suddenly I was awake and alert. Terrified, I tried to call on the name of Jesus. But I experienced the iron grip of evil and it was suffocating. I was held in a powerful grasp that seized me by the shoulders and wound around my body like a coil trying to squeeze the life out of me. It was so tight I could not even cry out the name of Jesus. I was like one dumb, able only to stutter out letters but never the full name of Jesus. I tried again and again and again. My heart yearned for relief as my body struggled against evil. This time—unlike the other times—I could actually feel the pain.

I don't know how long I struggled. I do know it seemed to go on and on as I writhed and twisted to break loose. At last I was free and I heard myself calling out the full name of Jesus. As I lay on my bed, I kept repeating that name silently in great relief. I looked at my arms, so conscious had I been of the pain, to see if there were any marks. I was afraid of looking—how awful it would have been to see any tangible signs of that struggle. No—I was much relieved.

I am writing now so that I may sleep in peace. And I asked Christ to grant me now his peace and to protect me.

Lord—I, your servant, am afraid.
But my heart is steadfast.
Now I remember what you said to me—
"Be firm and let your heart be steadfast."
I knew I was strong and brave and confident—
what did you mean?
Oh now, Lord, I understand!
To be exposed to such attacks
requires not bravery
but steadfastness.
Oh Lord, I am still afraid
when I am in those clutches,
for I experience destruction.
And yet, I know I will not be destroyed.
Evil holds no power
against a soul
that calls upon your Name.
But what force and power Evil has!
I tremble, I struggle—
and yet I cannot cry.
How long will it be
before I can call your Name?
When will you deliver me?
Oh God—look upon your servant!
Oh God—come to my aid!
Oh God—make haste to help me!
I will be steadfast.

Oh Lord—I, your servant,
call upon your Name.

"Put God's armor on so as to be able to resist the devil's tactics. For it is not against human enemies that we have to struggle, but against the sovereignties and the powers who originate the darkness in this world, the spiritual army of evil in the heavens." (Ephesians 6:11–12)

There is evil in the world. But God's love is more powerful.

August 9, 1979 — 11 AM

Stunned, I went into the chapel,
into the corner—quiet, dim,
lost in the shadows.
There, in the cool silence,
feeling bewildered and lost,
I bowed my head,
and my face ran wet with tears.
No words, no sound,
only silent weeping
heaving from the soul.
Yes, I am afraid.

Let me be steadfast,
Oh, let me be steadfast!
I am pitted against a power
unseen and evil.
My soul cries to the heavens
to the silent watchers and guardians of the night!
Oh, let me be steadfast!

I am here.
I have never left you.

But, where, where were you
when a grip like death
squeezed and clutched my life breath?
Oh where? Where were you?

I was there.
I was beside you,
watching,
loving,
weeping.
This must be so—it must be so,
for darkness has seen your love
and howls with rage against you.
Evil must visit you
to torment and taunt,
but it has no power over you
and cannot harm you,

for I am there,
and I will not leave you.
Evil can disturb your sleep,
destroy your peace,
throw you to the terrors of the night,
but no more.
Evil cannot destroy you,
for you are mine,
and I will protect you.
And when evil tires
of taunts and torments
it will leave you,
and I will hold you safe,
and in peace.

Be brave,
be steadfast,
do not be afraid.
This must be.
And your faith
will be strengthened,
your confidence will grow,
for I have conquered evil,
and you too
shall conquer evil
through me.
You are to learn
that there is no power

in the universe
deeper and greater
than love.

Many words of consolation and comfort
falling, falling with the tears
that also fell.
And slowly my soul stirred
and awakened to the light.
The sun, the gentle sun,
streamed into the shadows.
I moved as if from a deep sleep—
aroused—called softly by Love
with words of hope.

And I left, treading softly,
afraid to disturb my new awakening,
out into the day—
the beautiful day.
Sky—blue blue blue—
and light—dazzling and dappled—
on the young leaves.
I was alive,
and God—my God—
ran with me.
And I laughed
like a young child—freed.

August 12, 1979

It is almost time to leave, and I wonder at how the finger of God has traced my days. I have no doubt that these three months have been a time of preparation. During this period God has taken me aside and whispered:

Come, come here with me and I will show you
a desert place where you shall have a glimpse of
my wisdom
and you will see
the wonder of my ways.
And there I shall speak to you,
and whisper to your heart.
I will reveal to you a glimpse of my plan for you.
There, gently and with love,
like a dove with her chick,
will I hold you and feed you
my choicest food, my finest wine.

And as we sit and eat together,
I will unfold for you
the mystery and the beauty
of my love.
Together we will laugh and cry.
Together in the morning sun
we will rejoice and sing.
Together in the evening's cool

we will walk hand in hand,
silent in a love beyond words.
Together in the thick horror of the night
we will suffer and dispel
evil's marauding
and deepest rage
at our blossoming love.
And evil must attack
what it most fears.
But where it attacks
there I am
to hold you up, sustain you,
love you even more.

Ah, this time will be ours!
Like a secret—filled with hidden joys—
none will sound the depth
of my whispers in your heart.
None will measure the love
with which I cover and clothe you.
Impatient for the dawn will our love be—
reaching out in joy to the day
that blesses us with its hours
of silent sweet sharing.
Bless the day we walk together!
Bless the night we weep together!
Lovers lost—hidden in a place
that none can discover nor penetrate.

Like the rose, a splendid bud
gradually stirring, unfolding
before the gentle sun and breeze,
come—open—open!
Let me taste the fragrance.
And my eyes rest
on the very center and life force
of your beauty!
Come, rose—my flower—
for my words will gently persuade
and enfold you,
that you may open to the fullness
and radiance of the sun,
that you may absorb its riches,
stored and saved for you.
Come, rose—my flower—my beloved,
for long have I watched
and fed this tiny blossom,
and long have I yearned
for its fullness and its fragrance.
Come—come,
this time is ours,
to love, to hold, to weep together.
Come—loved one, come,
that in my garden
there might flower
a rose
that I have kissed.

God took me by the hand
and led me.
God showed me the mighty hills and said:
  See my footstool.
God showed me the vast desert and said:
  See the carpet beneath my feet.
God showed me the great rocks and pinnacles
and said:
  See where my finger rests.
And then God turned and looked at me
and said:
  See, see,
  the child—the loved one
  in whom I rest and live.

I have come to know and love God as never before. Now truly am I a prisoner in God's love; for there is nothing else for which I hope or long; nothing now to satisfy me except God. This love has overpowered and mastered me with a sweet and gentle strength. This love has shown me that my life can be spent only in serving love—totally and without reserve. So will my life be—to do God's work and to produce fruit a thousand-fold. God has whispered to my heart:

You are mine and mine alone.
Go, my love—my beloved—
in my name.

And I shall wait for you,
I shall wait for you,
and oh,
how I shall love you!

"Do not be afraid, you will not be put to shame, do not be dismayed, you will not be disgraced... I did forsake you for a brief moment, but with great love I take you back. For the mountains may depart, the hills be shaken, but my love for you will never leave you and my covenant of peace with you will never be shaken." (Isaiah 54:4, 7, 10)

This was my last reading the night before I left Algeria.

Praise be to God. Alleluia!
May this be only the beginning.
— August 18, 1979

CHAPTER FIVE

MOVING ON

My three months in the Sahara desert led me to a deep awareness that it was time to move on, that God was calling me to let go of my place in London as director and leader of the Volunteer Missionary Movement to continue the journey elsewhere.

I did not want to leave England. I had always loved my country. And I did not want to leave the VMM. I struggled with this call. But the certainty came from my time in the desert. The words I had heard were so clear to me: "I will never leave you but you must be faithful to the call." It was listening in the silence of the desert, and the prayer experiences I had there that gave me the trust and confidence to do what, otherwise, I would never have had the courage to do, which was to let go of so much that was central in my life.

I remember telling the cardinal about my decision to leave and go to the United States. But the cardinal disagreed with my decision. His words to me at that time were, "I order you to remain here in the Church in England and to work with me for the Church here." I remember being so convinced of my calling that I responded by saying that my faithfulness was first to the Spirit of God and that I had to respond to that call. In the end, the cardinal, who was a good and holy man, simply answered, "I can say nothing."

He knew I had to go.

I chose the United States specifically because of its distance from England. I knew that if I stayed close to England I would be tempted to return, but America was far away. I chose to study theology in Chicago because, after all those

At our second VMM House in London, 1977. Cardinal Hume was urging me to stay, but I had another mission, however unknown, in the United States.

years as an independent Catholic laywoman involved in creative ministry, I wanted to know more about theology and the Church's teachings. And at that point I was thinking I would just go for a year (to show my willingness?!)—and I would return as soon as possible to England to continue my work with the Volunteer Missionary Movement. Had I known then that this journey would take me to a place where I would spend the rest of my life, in exile from my own country, I would never have had the courage to set out on it. As always, I poured out my feelings in poetry:

Leaving and Following

Gently,
my soul quietly,
undramatically
is disturbed.
Who, what,
whispers in my soul?
Will this God of mine
not forget,
nor be satisfied?
What more, now,
does God ask
to intrude upon
my comfort and serenity?
I have given

this, that, and the other.
Will I have no rest
until this God of mine
has my soul and life-breath?
But how I treasure,
in silent satisfaction,
my lifestyle
and all its accoutrements!
How happily I possess
my home in London,
decorated so tastefully
and so well.
How I delight
in the comfort and pleasures
and company
I have gathered around me!
What would you
trade these for,
my God?
Will you continue
to run your finger,
gently,
over these smooth waters
moving around me?
Will you disturb
my tranquility
longer, my God?
Or will this be

a passing shadow,
moving mysteriously
over my soul
and receding
into nothingness?

Letting Go

It is time to go.
I can smell it,
Breathe it,
Touch it.
And something in me
Trembles.
I cannot cry,
Only sit bewildered,
Brave and helpless,
That it is time.
Time to go.
Time to step out
Of the world
I shaped
And watched become.
Time to let go
Of the status
And the admiration.

Time to go.
To turn my back
On a life that throbs
With my vigor
And a spirit
That soared
Through my tears.

Time to go
From all I am
To all I have
Not yet become.
I cannot cry,
But tremble
At the death
Within me,
And sob—
Tearless—
At the grief
That heaves
My soul.

Time to go.
Lonely,
Brave departure
That stands
Erect and smiling

While my very being
Shudders
In utter nakedness.

In September 1979, I flew from London to Chicago, leaving behind the Movement that had brought me so much struggle—yet so much joy and fulfillment.

A Lament on Leaving the VMM

Chicago, May 1980

I love you! I gave you birth in great pain. Do you remember? You were my pride and joy! Now you are fully grown and have become far greater than I. I can no longer hold you close to my heart like a child in need of care. Your life has flowered—powerful and all-embracing—and you stretch forward into the future. How I have loved you! And oh, how I have given my life and breath for you! And as I watched, startled, proud yet anxious at your phenomenal growth, I began to see that your looming shadow must cover me. Now, I hide and weep beneath your mantle.

Oh, how I love you still! Though I have gone, and I watch from far away your growth and becoming, yet I can never forget you, nor cease to be your mother. But now you birth your own children and they follow you, hundreds of them, tugging at your skirt. I must watch, silent and strangely sad, trying to be brave. But within me the tears are hot and in tiny little knots the veins around my heart contract.

Oh, how I have loved you! Do you remember me? Tell me—do you remember me? And do you cry alone and brave at my memory—as I do at yours?

I had to do all for you in the beginning. I cherished you with a mother's love, but, oh, you brought me such anguish! I had to stay with you to know what you would become, although you almost destroyed me. And so I stroked and kissed you, answered your every need. And I had to show those who resisted your becoming that you were in fact a blessing whose time had come.

CHAPTER SIX

CATHOLIC THEOLOGICAL UNION, CHICAGO

I studied in Chicago at a seminary called the Catholic Theological Union and graduated with a degree in theology. It was an important time and it was very good for me to study scripture, theology, and the history of the Church. I was privileged to learn from some of the finest teachers of theology and scripture. I am indebted to them for the insights that opened up for me a wider and deeper vision of my faith tradition. One teacher in particular was a gentle and distinguished senior scholar—Fr. Carroll Stuhlmueller—whose field was the Old Testament. I took his courses on the psalms and the Hebrew prophets.

Through Carroll's interpretation, the psalms became alive and even contemporary for me. The passionate love of God for the constantly erring people of Israel spoke powerfully to me of how, still today, the Christian community fails and rebels in spite of its avowed love and faithfulness! And

God, like a frustrated and angry parent, berates and rants and raves—through the prophets. But then, again and again, God relents, forgives, and welcomes back. One cannot but love and even feel empathy (!) for such a compassionate and immediate God. I learned to love the prophets who were the mouthpieces of God. I knew, without a doubt, that the prophetic call was not over. I was to be one of many—past and present—simply because God never gives up on God's people. The fact that the words of the prophets and of the psalmist are written for the most part in poetic form only intensified the emotional impact they had on me. Their language spoke to the human heart—and very much to mine.

My scripture teacher was Fr. Donald Senior, a noted scholar and writer, who broke open the gospel for me in a whole new way. Don presented insights on stories in the New Testament that took them beyond the purely written word. His exegesis revealed cultural and historical facts that opened up the scriptures for contemporary interpretation. The gospel came alive!

Fr. Larry Nemer taught Church history and also became a good friend. Along with lots of other historical facts, I learned that the Church I love (like the people of Israel) does not always do the right thing. There were stories of corruption and abuse of power as the Church grew and became rich and politically strong. The theme was familiar—human institutions and human beings, in spite of being graced and filled with the presence of God—were eminently prone to sin. And God was, and is, eminently prone to forgiveness.

I became more conscious of how God constantly calls us to justice and, in particular, to a "preferential option for the poor"—a theme that arose persistently from the liberation theologians of Central America. Catholic Theological Union did not neglect the primary importance of social justice as a vital aspect of being Church. The school offered programs and classes that focused on service, ministry, justice and peace.

It was at the seminary that I met Marie Claude Barbour, a professor of urban and social studies who introduced us to the poverty of the surrounding urban black communities. I was able to visit such communities and even ended up helping the people there dig and cultivate the earth and grow vegetables in tiny city garden plots.

Fr. Depaul Genska was a fellow student who had first encountered women involved in prostitution in New York. He initiated a "Night Ministry" in which students were invited to walk in the red light district of Chicago. I did. Often. I had no idea then that this was only the beginning of what was to become a whole new area of ministry for me, a ministry that would engage me and be my passion for the rest of my life. My occasional forays into the red light district of Chicago became, eventually, a lifelong journey with women involved in a lifestyle of prostitution.

But the seminary was a distinctly male institution. It had only recently allowed women to enroll and we were very much in the minority. One of the big issues talked about was the ordination of women. From where I was coming—Europe and British Catholicism—the ordination of women was not an issue. It was something I had never really got involved with, because I felt strongly about laity and was more concerned with the inclusion and empowerment of laypeople in the Church than I was with women's ordination. Consequently, the kinds of activities that went on in the seminary with regard to ordination and the place of women at that time held no interest for me. I remember being involved in a debate where I said that lay involvement was much more important than women's ordination. The role of the laity really was my issue.

Perhaps I felt a little smug about not jumping on the women's ordination bandwagon. But God was about to teach me a lesson—that all forms of exclusion are unacceptable to a just and loving God...

It was a lesson that I began to learn one night after I had had an exhausting day. At about 3 AM I was lying in bed in my little room in Student Housing both wide awake and tired. I had been trying to fall back to sleep, but my mind was utterly alert. Suddenly I experienced an inner urging that I could not deny. Reluctantly I got out of bed, stumbled to my desk, switched on my lamp, took a pad of paper and a pen, and began to write. I wrote fast and furiously—hardly conscious of the words that were tumbling out of me. Suddenly it was done. I climbed back to bed and fell fast asleep.

The following morning I looked at what I had written in those early hours. I was astounded and deeply moved:

The Anointing

There were no crowds at my
    ordination;
the church was cold and bare.
There was no bishop to bless and
    consecrate,
no organ music filled the air,
no solemn procession went before me,
no cross nor incense smell.
There were no songs nor incantation,
and no pealing triumphant bell.

But I heard the children laughing
in the stench of the city slums.
And I heard the people sobbing
at the roaring of the guns.
And the stones cried out before me
as the sirens wailed and roared.
And the blood of women and children
in the arid earth was poured.

There were no crowds at my
    ordination;
the church was cold and bare.
But the cries of the people gathered
and the songs of birds filled the air.

The wind blew cold before me,
the mountains rose and split.
The earth, it shuddered and trembled
and a flame eternal was lit.

There were no crowds at my
    ordination;
the church was cold and bare.
But the Spirit breathed oh so gently
in the free and open air.
She slipped through the walls and the
    barriers,
and from the stones and the earth
    she proclaimed:
Oh, see! My blind, blind people,
see Woman—
whom I have ordained.

There is not only one issue. All matters of injustice and exclusion must be our concern. God is big. We, too, must grow, be stretched, and allow ourselves to be transformed.

CHAPTER SEVEN

THE CALL

I wanted to return to England after I got my degree in theology, but, once again, I had this feeling inside of me—the same feeling that I had had at critical junctures and turning points in my life before. I felt strongly that God was trying to tell me something, trying to get through to me. I was deeply disturbed. It was close to graduation time and I remember that I was in a Church history class when I experienced such inner turmoil that I had to leave the classroom. I had a strong sense that I needed to get out of the city and spend time with God. There was a monastery on the outskirts of Chicago and I called and asked if I could go there for a few days. Something deep inside me was driving me to do this.

The monks told me that the retreat center would be closed for the next few days, that they did not have any guests, and that it would probably be too lonely for a woman alone. My response was, "That's exactly what I need!"

I was given a room in the retreat center attached to the monastery. I was totally alone and spent the next three nights in prayer.

During these nights I experienced a powerful awareness of the presence of God. St. Teresa of Avila appeared to me in a vision.

I'm really quite a practical, down-to-earth person, which is why I haven't shared any of these visions and dreams and experiences before, but I cannot deny or ignore them. It was during the encounters with Teresa of Avila that I came to realize what I had to do next. And perhaps that is why the whole thing had to be so traumatic. Had I not had such a powerful experience, I might simply have said, "It's time to go home." But I didn't go home to England, for the call I heard alone in the monastery at night was too real to be dismissed.

Perhaps the only way to express it is to share what I wrote during that time:

Dialogue with Teresa of Avila

May 11, 1980

I stayed awake to pray during the night and, as I knelt in the darkness, I became aware of a presence that seemed to surround me. Gradually I realized that it was Teresa of Avila who had joined me in that small room as a sister, filled with compassion and wisdom.

T. I have been waiting for you.

E. I have been looking for you.

T. Come to me, for I am your mother and your sister, and I am to hold your hand and guide you. I am to lead you gently through the light and darkness that once was mine and now is ours. I have been waiting for you to come, for God told me you would come when you were ready and asked me to care for you and lead you. I will be with you as you walk new paths in places you may fear. I will stand by you during all the encounters that lie before you. For God has given me charge. You must not be afraid. God loves you with a great love and that is why you are given special care and guidance, for I have walked this path before you. I know its darknesses and its pains. But you will never be alone. I shall walk this journey with you to the very end.

E. I am a child. I do not know where I am going. I only know you have crept into my life like a miracle and I have turned to you and cried aloud, "Teresa, help me! Be with me!" For I know in my soul I must go your way and your path is mine. And so I call aloud to you. I feel

I know you, so much of you is in me—your humor, your love of people, your longing to live and die for God. Ah! I smiled and loved you the moment I heard of you! I have loved you for your life and your joyfulness, your boldness and your laughter, and in all of that, I am so deeply aware of an intense and powerful love that drives you and would drive me. I need a companion on my way, Teresa, I need your warm hand and the reassurance of your shadow. I will come. I will take your hand. Take me with you.

T. I will not take you. I will come with you, for it is your path, though once it was mine. Now it is yours, uniquely yours. You are blessed and so loved. This path is one of great beauty, though it is lonely and climbs steeply. There are resting places, though few. I am so happy to walk with you. With the love and pride of a mother I will hold you up and comfort you. Though you fall, I will reach for you and hold you until you are strong enough to walk again. Do not be afraid, we are two.

E. This is a moment of great joy for me. I know our paths are one and for you I have a special love. I am no longer afraid. I feel so safe in your shadow. You will walk with me and we will sing, and sometimes cry.

T. Together we will do many things. We will laugh, for we both know how to laugh. We will run and be free, for the world is ours. In darkness we will come before our God, waiting for God's gentle light. You are pilgrim. Lover. Child of light. Beloved. Come!

The night spent with Teresa of Avila deepened my certitude that God was calling me to spend time alone so that I might listen deeply to the whispers in my soul. Teresa helped me to have the courage to say "yes" to that which I did not understand. I had to be faithful to the journey.

And now I knew I was not alone.

On reflection I considered that here was a woman who had gone through similar experiences that spoke to me because of my own. She was a woman of her time who ended up leaving her monastery at the call of God in order to take a very difficult journey to other parts of Europe to found new Carmelite monasteries.

I felt I, too, was a woman on a journey being called to start things, and to be both contemplative and active. That may be why I ended up with a vision of Teresa of Avila who became a guide for me, and promised that she would be with me throughout this new part of my journey.

The Trailer

The experiences I had were so totally convincing that there was not a shred of doubt in my mind that God was calling me to do something I had never even contemplated. And that was basically to do nothing. I was not to return to England and work for the cardinal, even though I wanted to do that. I was not to return to Africa. I was not to go back to the Volunteer Missionary Movement. I was to take time in the forest, or wherever—to be alone and to listen.

That, I think, is one of the hardest things of all, to be so nebulous and so vague, simply saying, "I'm called to do nothing," in a culture that is defined by productivity, achievement, and activity, and in which our credibility is often contingent upon what we do. I was about to graduate with a degree in theology (studies for which the cardinal archbishop of Westminster had paid), and I was saying, "Well, I'm going to do nothing now. This is my calling!"

Had I not had the visions in the monastery, had I not had such intense prayer experiences, I would never have come to such an apparently strange decision. But I knew I had to find a place to live in solitude, in quiet, and I knew this beyond question. There were, of course, other questions. I had once spent three months in the desert, but where was I to live now? And for how long? These questions had to do with practical matters. But with regard to the calling itself, there was no question at all.

Just before this time, one of the missionary societies in Chicago had approached me asking about the possibility of starting the Volunteer Missionary Movement in the United States. My answer had been no, that I had not been called to found the VMM here in the US. I had wanted to go back to England! But when I began to realize that I had to stay in the United States for a time of solitude, it seemed to me that perhaps this missionary society could be part of that, for they had told me that if I were to start the VMM here, they would let me use the property and land that they owned but were not using outside Chicago.

When I went to see this property in Yorkville, Illinois, and I saw the huge expanse of land that surrounded it, the experience was for me an "Aha!" moment. At first I wasn't really thinking of the foundation of the VMM. I was looking at the *forest* that surrounded the property, and my thought was that I could live here! Then it dawned on me that, at the same time, the opportunity was also being provided for the foundation of the VMM in the United States. The two things would happen at once: VMM could begin a new foundation and I would be the hermit in the woods, living out my call to solitude and spending time in prayer!

I contacted two lay missionaries in England and suggested that they might come to the United States, live in the house and start the VMM here. I would find myself a trailer, set it up in the forest, and pray for the VMM while I was there.

That is exactly what happened. A small group of VMM missionaries, four from England and two from the United States, came to live in the house that belonged to the religious community. They began VMM USA. I bought an old trailer and had it put in the forest. It did not have any connections or hookups for water or electricity, but I knew that it was sufficient.

The Forest

The call to live in the forest was a call to discover a much deeper part of myself—that of the contemplative solitary, which I felt had been submerged in my very active lifestyle. I felt powerfully moved by the lines from a hymn we sang at the VMM:

> "Long have I waited for your coming home to me,
> and sharing deeply our new life."

I heard those lines in my head and that rhythm, time and time again, as I prepared to move into my trailer in the forest. I also heard the words:

> "Be not afraid, for I am with you.
> Come, follow me, and I will give you rest."

This is what I believe God was doing, saying,

> "Come now, I want you for myself alone."

And I felt with St. Paul who wrote:

> "As for me, my life is already being poured away as a libation and the time has come for me to be gone. I have fought the good fight, I have run the race, I have kept the faith."

God did not have to shout any longer. God did not have to whisper anymore. For I had heard, and what I had heard was consistent and sure. I was saying my "yes" now, not because I had to, but because I wanted to, with everything that was in me. I wanted to be whole, I wanted to be faithful, but above all, I wanted to walk with my God.

The invitation had been there from the very beginning. I was not saying yes to something new. I was saying yes to the next part of an unfolding journey—a journey that had begun a long time ago. I could see only just so far ahead. The vision was not completely clear, and the way was partly shadowed, but God's powerful presence in the ground of my being was what urged me to say yes. I had fought the good fight. Now I was a pilgrim, a hermit—looking for the way.

I wrote a letter to Maria, my soul sister, who had taken over the leadership of the VMM in London:

> November 1981
> Well, here I am, in the middle of nowhere it feels! It all looks rather romantic—a clearing in the forest and a little trailer—but I think it is going to be difficult for me. I must get used to being alone with nothing exciting to do. It's going to take a lot of faith to stay with it—believing deep down that it all makes sense and will bear fruit sometimes, somehow. I am fasting for two days a week. Don't know how I'll ever get used to that! (God, I could do with an enormous toasted sandwich and a large gin and tonic!) I really don't feel that much kinship with the old ascetic lifestyle. Give me a bit of the good life, good food, and a party any time! I don't think I'll ever be like those ascetic hermits one reads about in Church history—all skinny and humble and holy, and totally at peace with poverty. I think I will always go for the joys and fun of

life. But here I am—the reluctant hermit. (Thanks, God!) Well—I'd better go and get on with praying Compline and drinking cocoa (erk)...

At the beginning of the trailer time, there was a real sense of excitement mixed with a strong inner call. I drew up a schedule for my day: getting up early and praying, living simply, reading the Hebrew Bible, and walking through the woods. I even prepared the ground for a small garden where I would grow vegetables and a few flowers. And I chopped and gathered wood for my little stove that served as the source of heat in the trailer.

As the days went by, the solitude and the loneliness became more challenging. And my prayer and contemplation were interrupted with times of dryness and emptiness and a feeling of being somewhat silly, wandering the woods alone! I know I'd been hoping that there would be some kind of revelation, or vision, or dream. I was accustomed to those kinds of things—I had already experienced them—but what happened in the forest was very different. On the whole it was not a time of great consolation and inspiration. Rather, it was most often a time of boredom and frustration. It was as if suddenly the God I knew and the visions I had experienced were things of the past. They had all disappeared and I could not find them anymore. I thank God for the deep-seated faith that kept me believing.

Throughout these weeks and months I did not experience the presence of God. I knew about being faithful. And I knew, intellectually, at least, that my call was true. I had to trust that God was there even when—especially when I could not see. I had to trust that Teresa was also with me as she had said she would be. Much of the time in the trailer was a dark time, a time of emptiness. As I walked through the forest I had to find the presence of God in the creation around me, rather than within me.

When winter came it was much more difficult, because the temperature sometimes went below zero. At night my little trailer would be very, very cold. It is hard to feel joy and inspiration when one is cold. But I stayed there, month after month, waiting for God. I wrote in my journal:

> Prayer is lifeless and much of the time I doze off. I am mechanically doing all I must—the simple round of collecting wood, lighting the fire, preparing beans, cleaning up, and feeding the cat. I also do some reading from the Bible, sit silent before God, and pray the Office. Outside, the snow begins to fall, the temperature drops. I feel eccentric and a little ridiculous. God is silent. And I, too, wait in silence and pray that I may be steadfast.

The amazing thing is that somehow I had the fortitude to hold on. Somehow I had the courage not to give up.

And somehow I had the faith to believe. By the time the seventh and the eighth month came I was literally holding on to nothing. It was in the ninth month that I began to experience God's call again and to feel a renewed awareness of God's presence. It was a powerful reassurance—after months of nothing, having God burst forth from that dark space! And I began to think of a woman who conceives a seed of new life within her, and of how she must undergo a period of gestation and waiting as that new life grows. And I realized that this is what God does with us. Although we cannot see, the invitation is to trust in the darkness and to wait for the surfacing of God's wisdom in our lives by allowing the gestation period to happen.

How easy it is for us to give up in frustration when we feel abandoned or alone or think that God does not hear us. How desperate we are to have control and to know what's going on and to have answers as we try to discover what God wants us to do! Maybe what we need is simply to realize that God does not hide from us, ever, but that God gestates within us—the grace of God gestates within us—and we must be faithful to the spiritual process of birthing the presence of God into our world.

And so for me, it was with deep gratitude that I knew I had been given the fortitude and the grace to stay in the forest, waiting for the emergence and the surfacing of God's call. The gestation was over.

It was time to find a midwife.

My trailer in the forest. I had no water or electricity and waited nine months to hear God's call. Then I knew: it was time for a midwife.

The Retreat

By the end of June 1981 I knew I needed someone to walk with me during the final weeks of this journey. I knew I needed someone with wisdom and experience in discernment. I was blessed to find a Jesuit priest who was offering a thirty-day Ignatian retreat in Illinois. His name was Father Jim Doyle.

Jim was my midwife. He walked with me during thirty days of prayer and struggle. He listened with complete openness and receptivity to the dreams and visions I experienced during that retreat. He accepted without question the revelations I was blessed with, in particular those from Mary and Teresa of Avila. These two women became my constant companions and, along with Father Jim, they helped guide me toward a clear understanding of my call.

During the final days of my nine months of prayer I knew without a doubt that I was being called to work in the inner city, to reach out to women involved in a life of prostitution. It seemed to me that my journey and my experiences of the last few years had all been leading me to this point. How else could God have brought me to an awareness of such a call? How could my realization of it not have been preceded by so much longing, darkness, seeking, and, ultimately, a vulnerability that led me simply to say "Yes"? It was only in deep silence that I came to hear the whisper of God.

I knew, without any doubt by then, that I was not to live again in England—the country that meant so much to me and held so many wonderful memories. God had led me into a place of exile and I had been seduced. I went back to visit my family and my hometown and sat, once again, in the shadowy silence of the cathedral where I had heard the first call.

Lancaster Cathedral

Here I am—
home again—
within your worn
grey walls,
a little scrap
of dazed humanity
sitting
blanketed and protected
beneath
your soaring spire,
carrying into
the universe
the whispered prayers,
cries, and tears
of millions
who sought refuge—
as I do,
like a child
curled
in your stony womb.
Here,
in this great, great cathedral
I am home,
and every stone,

every aged pillar,
every gold-embossed
wing of angels,
knows
that I am here
where my soul
was born
to be carried
into the world,
then to return
with whisperings
of love
into the caress
of your Great Bosom.

CHAPTER EIGHT

THE STREETS

It is not necessary at this point to go into all the practical details of how I began my new mission. Suffice to say I ended up in the city of Chicago, where I rented a room and simply began to walk the streets at night. It was of course often a scary experience—I was unfamiliar with street culture and unprepared for the depth of poverty and loneliness I encountered in the homeless, the winos, the mentally disabled, and the unemployed. But I was deeply aware that God was present in the heart of the pain and the chaos that I saw. I knew that God walked with me on those dark and dismal streets.

It is fitting at this point to share what I wrote in my journal at that time:

> Yesterday I spent all day walking around the streets in Chicago. I felt afraid and very small, and I wished I had someone to talk to about that. The streets are cold and impersonal, often dark and frightening. Am I a coward?

I had a thought yesterday—just a crazy, selfish thought—of getting on a plane and going home to England. I wanted to run—to disappear—to forget all this. I know I won't—but I know I'll dream and think those thoughts again. I am not so strong and so brave as people think.

I talked to the women on the streets, the homeless, the winos, the lost, and I am deeply moved by the pain and hopelessness. The women involved in prostitution share their stories with me. I am both honored and devastated:

> "I would just do it to hurt myself. I hated my father. It was one way of getting back... Hurting myself maybe would hurt him."

> "I was lonely. I had no one to come home to. I had to have someone to come home to. Having even a pimp is better than having nobody."

> "I switch off. Don't think about it."

> "...to have someone who really cares...really loves you...just someone who would put their arms around you and hold you...even if he does beat you sometimes."

> "You think you are just a piece of shit. The guys are all pieces of shit..."

> "I was never allowed to be my own person. I never learned how to make decisions for myself. My pimp did everything for me—I didn't have to worry about anything."
>
> "Some people hit food, some people hit drink—when I am depressed and lonely, I turn tricks. What difference does it make?"
>
> "I would never have talked to a person like you. How could I—on welfare and a prostitute—talk to you? Why would you want to talk to me?"

I am learning fast that the women we criminalize for prostitution have as much need as any of us for love and understanding. Often all they get is abuse and jail. Almost all the women I have met and talked to, so far, were abused way back when they were just children. Their world has been one of violence. They have always confused love and abuse and many times equate the two. Why don't we understand?

I also befriended some of the street winos. One man, named Mark, had been drinking on the streets of Chicago for nearly twenty years. Yet beneath all his external grime and shabbiness I discovered a true gentleness and sensitivity. Mark even became part of our small VMM community outside Chicago—he was a delight, bringing to our small group a sense of humor, a simplicity, and an authenticity that touched us all.

One day as I was walking through the forest at the VMM Center I noticed what appeared to be a table leg sticking out from underneath the bushes and the brambles. Someone must have dumped this table years ago and now it was all overgrown. As I investigated further, I noticed that the legs of the abandoned table were carved with what looked like grapes and vine leaves. It must have once been a very good table! I returned to the house and called Mark to help me pull it from beneath all the brambles. Together we carried it up to the garage. The table was painted bright red. "I'll fix it," said Mark, as he took a piece of broken glass and began to scrape. For weeks he scraped. Underneath the red paint he found green paint, so he continued to scrape. And underneath the green paint was brown paint. Mark continued to scrape.

It took almost six months. But eventually, there it was, a beautiful antique oak carved table in all its natural beauty! Mark leant on the table with pride. "It's beautiful, Mark!" I declared. "Let me go and buy some of that lemon oil furniture polish to finish it off!"

"No," responded Mark, "ain't gonna be nothing unnatural about this!" And he went out into the forest, gathered berries from the bushes, and brought the berries up to the house. He boiled them and made a natural berry resin. Then he covered the table in the resin. It was beautiful. As I looked at Mark and the table I felt God saying: "The table is Mark and Mark is the table."

With Mark, who taught me the power of kindness and grace.

God was teaching me that beneath all our masks and external covers, every human person is precious and beautiful!

All the encounters I had on the streets and in the bars and brothels left me numbed and hungry for hope and justice. One such instance was an encounter I had with a woman in a bar...

She started talking to me, opened her bag, took a loaf of bread and a can of tuna fish, and asked if I'd like a sandwich. How much more easily the poor share of the little they have! So we sat at the bar eating tuna-fish sandwiches. It was very dark and the music was loud. Anna talked. She cried. She said she was lonely and sad . . . a desperate woman. She talked about the men in her life who had used her and left her. She said she still worked as a prostitute and she asked me outright if I wanted to team up and work with her. I wasn't sure of how to respond, but in the end, I told her I was a minister. That took her by surprise—she didn't know whether to laugh or cry, but eventually decided to cry. Then, exhausted, she lowered her head, rested it on the bar counter, and fell asleep. I felt so helpless. There was nowhere to take her—no home—no shelter that was open at this hour. There were only the streets—always the streets. I just sat next to her, surrounded by all the noise and laughter of a bar, and felt so totally inadequate to

The streets of Chicago became my parish and my new cathedral.

help or to comfort. Finally I left her a note with the address of a shelter and walked away. In the darkness outside I pondered on how we had broken bread together and eaten together and talked about life and God. We had held each other. Eucharist had been broken and shared in that hellish place.

The streets of Chicago became my church. My congregation was made up of the winos, the drug addicts, the homeless, and the prostitutes. Every encounter, every moment spent sitting in the bars, the brothels, the streets, and the shelters became, for me, eucharistic events. I knew that God was there.

At the end of one Thanksgiving day I found myself at a brothel, sitting alone with the madam in a silent house after all the women and clients had left.

As winter darkness deepened around the gaudy street lamps and the traffic slowed with the oncoming night, May and I sat together at the now empty kitchen table. In the uncustomary quiet the little kitchen seemed suddenly stilled and vulnerable. The madam looked at me, and then she crumpled, weeping. I wrapped my arms around her frail, aged body. Then she spoke hoarsely from a place deep within. "Thank you... thank you for loving us," she sobbed. "We are so lonely. We are all so lonely."

In the darkening brothel, as I held the sobbing elderly lady, my heart ached. So this was why God had brought me here—to be with the people who were most rejected and misunderstood! I was simply to be present. I was simply to listen. And, deep in my heart, I understood that I was here for my own conversion. The people I was meeting and coming to love touched me deeply; I became conscious of a powerful sense of compassion rising from within me and I knew that God was hurting. I listened to the women's stories—all made mention of childhood abuse and violence. The women were all so deeply wounded that they were unable to heal themselves and so, it seemed, they no longer cared. But I knew they were precious in God's eyes and I knew that God grieved for them. My task was somehow to pass on the love and tenderness of God to these most broken women.

It worked both ways, though, because there is no question that the love and tenderness of God was also being passed on to me. One night as I was walking down the street I happened to glance across the road. A large grey church stood on the corner. Sitting on the steps of the church were five women. They were bag ladies. I could not quite make out what they were doing, but they were sitting in a kind of circle. The woman on the top step saw me and called out to me: "Come and join us—we're having a picnic!" I was somewhat surprised, given that it was around 9 PM and darkness was falling. But I walked over to the group and was promptly directed to sit down. On the middle step there was a large plastic bottle of ginger ale and a battered-looking box from Dunkin' Donuts.

The woman who was clearly the leader of the group declared loudly, "There's enough for everybody!" After placing polyester cups on the steps, she then proceeded to pour the ginger ale, measuring very carefully to ensure that each cup had the same amount of soda. Again she declared, "There's enough for everybody." She then passed around the cups to each of us and opened the box in which lay several stale donuts—clearly salvaged from the trash cans outside Dunkin' Donuts. Finally she broke one of the donuts, passed me half, distributed the others, and declared yet again, "There's enough for everybody..." We sat in silence—eating and drinking as darkness fell.

It was Eucharist.

After the ginger ale and donuts were finished, the women rose, gathered up the remnants and stumbled down the steps toward their waiting shopping carts filled with all their earthly belongings. They headed off into the night—looking for a shelter. I was left amazed and deeply humbled.

Experiences like these gave me a glance into another world where the grace of God was present even in such darkness and suffering. I knew that God was leading me, opening my eyes to a new consciousness, opening my ears to a new call to action and compassion.

This call became even clearer when I received a letter from a woman in jail, a letter that deepened my resolve to do something for women involved in prostitution.

Dear Edwina,

My name is Tracy Jones. I'm an unhappy prostitute of eight years. I have three beautiful children whom

I've been blessed to have and I'm now ten weeks pregnant again and it has left me in a deep depression whereas I don't wanna live anymore. I'm just tired and used up. I can't seem to get a start anywhere, but today someone told me about you and that gave me hope for a new life. If I fail this time then I shall kill myself.

I can't believe there is someone who really understands. See, I am very weak and I thought I was alone. See, my hooker friends never discuss the reality of working the streets. All we do is lie to each other. I truly have grown to hate the life. I'm so ashamed of what I am and I do wanna change. I have to. If I don't, I don't wanna live and I'm not bluffing.

When I first started to work the streets my eleven-month old girl was murdered by my pimp and this started me to using drugs so I wouldn't have to face the reality of what happened. It got to the point where drugs didn't help me anymore so I joined a drug program. Sure it helped me kick drugs but all of a sudden I was awake and can see what I have become . . . which is nothing, the scum of the earth.

I know no other way but the streets. I tried a shelter and at 6:00 in the morning they woke me and said I had to leave. That discouraged me and I turned tricks to pay for my room every day. You know what we learned about the street life is that no one can change unless they are truly fed up. You can't do it for your kids, or for your parents, but for yourself.

What I am asking for is a new life and I can't make it without the help of someone who knows exactly what I'm going through. See, I'm sick in the mind and I hurt just thinking of what I've been through. Now I'm doing seventy days in the Cook County Jail for stealing clothes for my kids and myself. I should be getting out next month and I'll be about four months pregnant then and I don't wanna go back to abusing myself. So I am going to need a place to stay temporary and someone to show me how to get on public aid. I don't have a Social Security card and that's gonna take time. In the meanwhile, I don't wanna turn tricks to survive.

I'm willing to work, scrub floors, and things just for your ear to listen and guide me and a place to lay my head. Without your help I don't think I can make it. I'll sleep on the floor.

See, I believe in God and Jesus Christ and if it wasn't for him spurring me on, one of my tricks would have killed me by now. I believe I'll be forgiven for my sins, but if I kill myself, then I'll never see my little girl in Heaven. Please, please, please help me so I can help myself. You are a blessing to hookers. I didn't think anyone cared, and even if you don't help me, just continue your good work. If you change or turn a few people in the right direction then your work is not in vain.

Prostitution isn't related to anything else. It is a sickness of its own, like cancer. Cancer is the root of the problem and it's the same with real hookers. We are a desperate kind of people, and prostitution is the root of our problem.

Please guide me. I'm not asking for charity. I'm willing to work for a bed to sleep in, temporarily, while I get public aid together. Please don't turn your back.

Thank you.

Tracy Jones

As I read this letter, I knew with certainty that I had to find a house—a house for women like Tracy.

CHAPTER NINE

GENESIS HOUSE

I had to find a place—a safe place where the women could come for healing and new life. Once again I was looking for a house!

I scoured the streets looking for "For Sale" or "For Rent" signs. Eventually I found what seemed a perfectly sized house in an ideal location—right opposite the train station and bus stops, and in the middle of the area where I walked. I called the realtor and made an appointment to see the property. Two of the women accompanied me to inspect the house. The realtor was not a little surprised and dismayed as he realized the kind of women who were checking out the property! But, when I told him I liked it and was very interested, he suggested that we meet in his office to discuss a contract. At this point I had to tell him that I had no money but that it would come because this was the house God wanted for us. The realtor looked confused and puzzled, but I assured him that everything would be all right.

Cardinal Joseph Bernadin and Catholic Charities eventually agreed to pay the rent for the house for an initial period of three years. God had provided! I called it Genesis House—a place of new beginnings from chaos—and in 1983 I moved in.

Slowly the "ladies of the night" began to come. My intention was to develop a house of hospitality where

Chicagoland

Chicago Tribune Sunday, May 19, 1985

Prostitutes find new beginning

By Wes Smith

She was 28 years old, well-educated and beautiful with dark eyes, long black hair and olive skin.

When Lt. James Crowley saw her weeping in the 23d District police headquarters, he knew she did not belong among the hundreds of street prostitutes who work in the Lakeview area of Chicago's North Side.

"She carried herself so well. I knew she was out of place here," Crowley said.

She was a Moslem from Morocco who came to Chicago to marry a local businessman she had met in her own country. It was an opportunity for a new life, she told Crowley.

But in her first days with her fiance, the modest Moslem woman was horrified. He showed her pornographic movies and ordered her to sell herself for sex on the streets for his profit.

"Even though this job hardens you, I couldn't help feeling sorry for her," said District 23 task force police officer Ed Tiedje.

Police took the frightened woman to a unique "house of hospitality" in the Lakeview area—a place where prostitutes are viewed as victims, not criminals; where they can escape, permanently or temporarily, from the world of drugs and alcohol and what one cop called "the most dangerous job on the face of the Earth."

"I feel if I can drop a girl off and she goes in those doors, she has walked a thousand miles," Crowley said.

This place, Genesis House, is one

Tribune photo by John Dziekan

A ceramic brothel with prostitutes waving from the windows decorates the mantel behind Edwina Gateley [left], who runs Genesis House, and Dolores "Teddy Bear" Lugo, who lives there.

of only three or four "prostitute retreats" in the United States, according to Margo St. James, founder of COYOTE, a prostitutes' rights group based in San Francisco.

The unique nature of Genesis House is attested to by its two chief sources of funding. Catholic Charities gives $1,000 a month toward rent and food, and an elderly madam, who runs a busy brothel down the street, chips in.

"They do an awful lot of good. I don't know if most people appreciate them, but I do," said the madam, who gives $30 to $100 a month.

Genesis House applies an innovative approach to an age-old problem. Inside comfortable rooms decorated by donation, you are likely to find priests and prostitutes,

Continued on page 3, this section

together we would become family. I knew that one of the major problems for the women was a sense of alienation and loneliness—nobody really cared for them. I felt that if we could create our own family, connecting and bonding with each other as sisters, this would provide a strong foundation for recovery. Jesus did not tell the people he met that they needed job training or social skills; he first welcomed and loved them and motivated them enough to believe in themselves. That is real freedom and dignity, the foundation for new life. That is how I wanted to do it. And that is what I did.

Genesis House became a model program for women recovering from prostitution in the Midwest. I was able to raise money by appealing in churches as well as speaking to women's groups all over the country. Genesis House grew. I began to see women turning their lives around and my heart rejoiced in the providence and goodness of God.

Genesis House was registered as a not-for-profit organization. A board was formed and staff members were appointed. I loved the women and admired their courage as they struggled in recovery. Our gatherings, meal times, and graduation ceremonies were a source of great joy and delight to me. I felt like a mother with many children. As the program grew I was able to spend more time doing public speaking, fund raising, and sharing the women's stories while counselors and social workers, as well as senior women in recovery, took care of the program.

The Shift

But with the appointment of a new executive director in 1996 I began to notice, with some apprehension, that things were beginning to change in my house of hospitality. The new leadership was not what I had hoped it would be. Hospitality and nurturing were no longer central. The residential program was reduced; women who were my graduates and who had been employed in the program were gradually let go of, and "professionals" were hired in their place. The staff changed radically from a team of caring people who empathized with the women in recovery and loved them, to a staff who, on the whole, were there for their salaries and the prestige of working in such a publicly admired program.

I found myself in the painful position of trying to advocate for the women and the charism of the program with a board now stacked with individuals who were friends and supporters of the new leaders. The pursuit of funding and rapid growth seemed to be the major preoccupations of this once charismatic and hospitable program.

For three years I struggled to keep the organization I had founded on track. It was possibly the most painful and heartbreaking time of my life. As the years passed, I watched the program diminish and change. Things reached the stage where I was no longer welcome in my own home. I was apparently too much of a threat to the new leaders. Eventually I was informed that I must never enter Genesis House again. The women were devastated. I was broken.

Where was God now?

How could this have happened?

But in spite of these painful questions, to which I did not have answers, I never doubted the existence of the One who had called me so many years ago. It was just a dark, dark time. Under incompetent leadership and financial mismanagement, Genesis House finally had to close its doors in 2006. I stood and watched as the house was emptied and the residents returned to the streets.

I was numb with grief. I fled into the woods to grieve alone and lament before my God. No one can measure the pain I experienced. There was no longer any home for these most broken women to find refuge in recovery. Why had I failed? I remembered how, years ago when I was a young missionary in Africa, a religious sister, for no apparent reason, looked at me intently and spoke with great conviction words I have never forgotten: "God has laid his finger upon you..."

Where was the finger of God now?

Where was it as Genesis House—a haven and house of healing for so many broken and wounded women—collapsed and closed its door, the door I had opened with such faith twenty-three years before?

April 2006

There are no obituaries
for the dying of my dream,
just a consciousness
of a space
filled with dull aching
and soul heaviness.
There are no ruins left
of this dying either,
just a few echoes—
some laughter,
some clapping—
bouncing around in my head,
mocking memories once so sweet.
It has been a long, long dying time,
and I have kept watch,
longing for a stirring of life,
and clutching a little hope
that death would slink away,
defeated by the dreamers.
But you were too long sick,
too weakened in spirit,
my lovely dream,
and when you died
beneath a brutal hand
I nodded dumbly,
almost grateful,

that my sad despairing watch
was over,
and I could finally say goodbye
and carry home,
to hold and kiss,
a few shining shreds,
of our great love affair.

VISION

Like a white moon
hung in a blackened sky
my vision shone—
clear and splendid.
Ah, how I loved it,
romanced and treasured it.
How I traced it lovingly,
caressed it and proclaimed it.
And all beheld
my vision clear
like a white moon
against night suspended.
But slowly
and so steadily,
shadows slid across
my well-loved vision
until it was no more

like a white moon
brightening
all it shone upon,
but only a night—
cold and comfortless.
How I grieve!
Oh! How I grieve
my vision
shadowed over.

The women who had gone through my program at Genesis House and who knew me and loved me gathered around in mutual grief. We met to pray together and to try to find a new way. I remember saying to them, "My dream has been destroyed."

One of the women replied, "Your dream has not been destroyed. We are your dream—and we are alive."

Those words continue to stay with me all these years later and indeed, there is a truth in them, for the women with whom I once shared my life now continue the journey in their own way, many working in the fields of recovery for others—in drug treatment programs, HIV programs, and homeless shelters. We are like the diaspora—a network of brave, courageous women continuing to believe in their dreams in spite of great adversity. We are still family—and our home is the streets.

I can see now that, for all the darkness of that time, God never left me:

Come.
Hide in me,
said God!
I have this huge,
huge shawl,
and, when you are
still enough
to let me hold you,
I will wrap you round
in warmth
and you will be
cocooned in love
and disappear in me.

Let me hold you
as you weep,
dear one,
for I am here with you.
When darkness wraps you round,
dear one,
so does my love
for you.
Those times you feel
you walk alone
your shadow is me,
dear one,

and when your heart
is tight with grief
I sing my song,
dear one.
It is a song of love
for you
sprung from my deep desire
to fill your soul
with peace,
dear one,
and soothe and heal
your pain.
So let me
hold you close,
dear one.
You'll not be left alone,
you'll hear my song
in the night,
dear one,
for I am
your love
and your home.

The darker it becomes the more we must trust that we are enveloped in a light that only blind faith can see.

God is with us.

CHAPTER TEN

MOTHERHOOD

In 1992, I was asked to consider adopting a newborn African American baby. I knew this would be impossible for me alone. But I had a close friend, Maureen, who was also a member of the Volunteer Missionary Movement and was working as my assistant/secretary. We were living together in a small community of missioners. Maureen immediately offered to share in the upbringing and mothering of the baby. During my travels and absences, which I came to acknowledge as my missionary journeys in the United Sates, it was Maureen who nurtured and cared for my son.

This was the beginning of a whole new journey for me. God was taking me farther than I would ever have chosen to go. The adoption presented a radical change in my lifestyle but, more than that, bringing up my son has brought me to a far deeper understanding of the love of God and the notion of the Motherhood of God than I could ever have imagined.

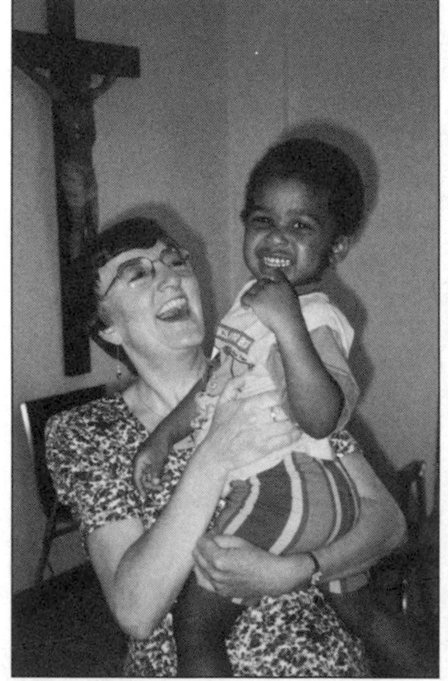

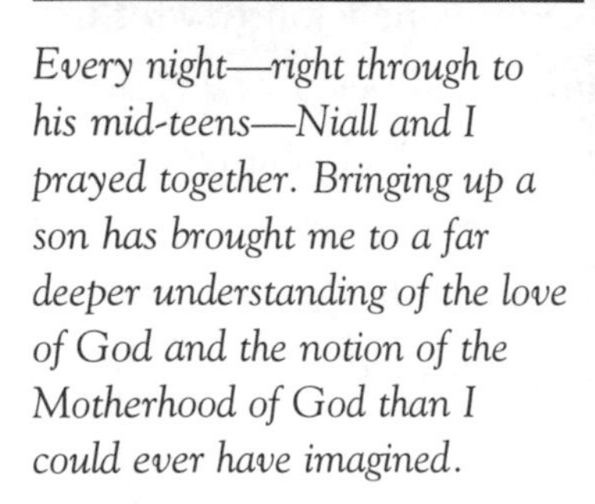

Every night—right through to his mid-teens—Niall and I prayed together. Bringing up a son has brought me to a far deeper understanding of the love of God and the notion of the Motherhood of God than I could ever have imagined.

From an early age, it was clear that my son suffered from what I believe to have been a prenatal condition. Being adopted has its own traumas and he experienced significant emotional distress. His early years were fraught with emotional ups and downs and moods swings. Suffice it to say that the years through to his teens were the most challenging and demanding of my life. This period was filled with meetings with doctors, counselors, teachers, and social workers—it was exhausting and, most of all, emotionally draining. But I love my son with a passion. Whatever it took to help him grow, develop, and find happiness had to be done. And so I began to understand what motherhood really meant. In my case, it meant giving all. Nothing was too much in the search to find help and nurturing for my son.

I wanted to bring my child up to have a notion of God that was bigger than the one I had been taught as a child. I wanted him to know that in my experience, God was not confined to any gender or position. God was not a man or a woman or a king or a lord or a judge. God was, fundamentally, love, and our task as humans was to manifest that love to the world through compassion, mercy, and justice. We, as my friend St. Teresa of Avila expressed so well, are to be the hands, feet, and eyes of Christ for the world today.

Every night—right through to his mid-teens—my son and I prayed together. We always prayed that the human family would care for the earth—our home—as well as each other. The prayers of a child are always powerful, and my son's early childhood prayers never failed to soften me:

> Thank you God for the beautiful earth you gave us to live on, even tho' we don't respect it. But my Mom respects it and I respect it. My cat doesn't understand and my kitten doesn't have a brain cell, and my dog's too old. But thank you, anyway, God for our beautiful world.

Being a mother brought a whole new dimension into my life!

I continued to earn a living by responding to the increasing numbers of invitations to give retreats and conferences throughout the country. I remembered my time in the desert where I became conscious of a call that would lead me to speak aloud and not to be afraid of sharing with others my journey with God. In spite of—or perhaps because of—all the struggles I had experienced with God's call, I felt impelled to speak about the amazing faithfulness of the One who continued to hold my hand. Even when I could not see, I knew that God was there. Even when I could not hear, I knew God could. Perhaps it was because of the intensity of my experiences in solitude that I could never imagine—not even in the worst moments—that God would totally abandon me.

I was conscious that God wrapped me around and rocked me in my pain, in my deep concern for my son and in my distress over the destruction of Genesis House. During this time I grieved over the fact that the women in recovery now had no place to go, no place to heal, no place to gather. I knew that such a place was vital for women's recovery and healing. I wrote a poem about it and shared the poem with a group of middle-class women who attended one of my retreats in Chicago:

A Place

I dream a place
for women
to come apart
to meet themselves
in a safe and nurturing space.

A place where women
who have never been alone
or looked upon
their deep feminine selves
can be free to sink
into the wombs of
their grandmothers,
their mothers,
themselves.

I dream a place
where all the cycles of
a woman's life

will be acknowledged
and celebrated
in tune with nature and
the rhythms of the earth.

I would like a place
where the weary,
the battered, and the raped
will find healing
in herbs and touch and dance.

I dream a place
where women will sing and chant
beneath the full moon
and dance around
the dying embers,
a place where the feminine
will be nurtured
and born again
into our world.

Ah, I dream a place
for virgin, mother, and crone
to rise again
in fullness with the moon.

Led by Carolyn Vogt Groves (who eventually became my close friend and soul sister) a group of women got together and started a small foundation to raise funds for the women of the streets to get out of the city and attend my retreats. We called it Sophia's Circle (Sophia being the ancient Greek word for the Wisdom/Spirit of God). A vital part of my program at Genesis House was to be resurrected! So began a new network based in Chicago, supported by donations from women all over the United States and offering ongoing nurturing and hospitality to women recovering from prostitution. We had no house, but I was able to use retreat centers operated mostly by religious communities. Two or three times a year we gathered (and continue to gather) in groups of about eighteen women in recovery to share, cry, heal, and pray. The dream was small (and sustained financially by a very limited budget) but it was very much alive! Sophia's Circle continues today to serve women in recovery from prostitution.

My life had now become a juggling act involving child care, public speaking, writing, and spending time with my network of women in Chicago and Sophia's Circle. Even in the midst of all this, however, I knew that my hunger and longing for solitude had to be met. I had to find a place to which I could retreat and pray in the midst of a very full life.

CHAPTER ELEVEN

THE HOUSE OF SOPHIA

I did not have the financial resources to buy a place—even a small one. But walking through the lovely lakeside property of the Benedictine Sisters of Erie one day I suddenly visualized a tiny cabin snuggled in the trees. What a beautiful place to hide, retreat, pray, and write! I became so excited by the idea that I decided to go for it. I wrote a letter to the Benedictine prioress asking if I could use a small corner of their property and build a little cabin. Imagine my delight when the reply came that the Benedictines "would be honored" to let me build a cabin/hermitage on their property!

All I needed now was the money to build the cabin! I sent a heartfelt appeal to everyone I knew, as well as to all the women who had attended my retreats. With the donations I received from wonderful people, plus a grant from Sophia's Circle and my own savings, I was able to pay for the building of a small wooden cabin. I called it The House of Sophia. Over the years it has served as a place of prayer

My cabin on the lakeside property of the Benedictine Sisters of Erie—again a silent corner of peace in God's Womb.

for women (and even some men) who sought silence, nurturing, and healing in the midst of our noisy and fast-moving world. For me, it became my refuge, my silent corner, my hiding place of "rendezvous" with God. I wonder now whether without this I could ever have survived, for my life was more than full with my call to motherhood, my grieving the loss of Genesis House, my writing, my ongoing ministry with the women in recovery, and my work of preaching and speaking to the Christian community. It was in the little cabin in the woods that God, yet again, was my great comfort. It was in the silence and solitude of The House of Sophia that I poured out my soul in poetry.

Here I am again...
Having fled from the world,
I bury myself
in silence
and am wrapped around
by the warm protective walls
of my little wooden cabin.
"It is safe here,"
I whisper,
all snuggled up with God.
Here I can find respite
from the noise and pain
I see
on city streets, TV screens,
and every corner where we
frightened humans gather
to grapple
with a world gone mad.
"Come, hide here,"
whispered God.
"Here, here!—
in this silent lonely place—
Come, here with me!"

"And"
(all conspiratorial),
God murmured tenderly,

"here we can
play nurses,
and hold the world together."

"Where have you been?"
asked God.

"Oh, around, around,"
I mumbled.

"Missed you,"
said God.

"But, now that you're here,
let me teach you
how to dance."

"I would like to walk with you,"
said God.
"We could even skip or run
or jump! We could play!
And don't worry if anyone sees you—
tell them that you were a little

drunk
and you got carried away
by love."

"Hush,"
God said to me
one day
in the midst
of my fervent prayer.
"Hush,
I can't hear
your breathing . . ."

These birds
just don't stop singing.
Their notes
spill out from every tree,
and a million leaves
shake with their
melody.
They must think
this is a cathedral
and the domed sky above
(gold with dying sun)

a masterpiece—
of Michelangelo, perhaps...
or of God
playing tricks.

On my altar
here in the forest,
there is no chalice—
but only a little mushroom
rooted in the aged
tree trunk
standing, it seems
with proprietary bearing,
amidst a small bundle
of nuts
covered with dying leaves.
Spiders, little beetles,
and a thousand
unseen living things
dance upon and within
my forest altar...
Yet for all its simplicity,
it is, for me,
as mighty a testimony
to the wonder and
fertility of God

as the most magnificent
marbled altar
swathed in gold—
but upon which
nothing grows
or dances.

I fall
into the rhythm
of my breath.
It is God's
silent lullaby
and I must sleep,
awake,
in its steady
flow
until I am
lost in it—
and gathered up
in the ocean of God,
to be then laid gently
on some distant shore—
still breathing.

Ah—my choir is here!
All the songbirds
of the forest
gather
to cheer and comfort me.
God—pouring music on the earth!
There cannot be
a more soothing balm
nor a more tender lullaby.
Generosity wraps me round.

I sat in the warm sand—
listening to the song
of the lake,
and, as I stretched in joy,
beneath the blushing sky,
I felt myself
cradled
and cupped
in God.

I felt, indeed I knew, that in The House of Sophia, I was in God's Womb.

CHAPTER TWELVE

PUBLIC SPEAKING

More and more I was being invited to lead conferences and retreats. Devoting my time to such activities became not only a source of income for my son and me, but also an opportunity to share with others something of my own personal journey with God. This could not be done without also speaking of the mandate given to every follower of Christ, the mandate to be involved in justice and peace. Prayer and ritual without a life committed to justice, peace, and the elimination of poverty is a sham. Spirituality and justice are inseparable. That is what the gospel of Jesus teaches us.

As wars escalated, poverty deepened, violence grew, and injustice continued unabated in our world, I increasingly came to feel that the Christian Church and we Christian people were failing abysmally in our calling to bring about the realm of God. It was, therefore, natural and imperative that in all my public speaking I would call for personal and global transformation.

I was extremely well received. My love of God, my spirituality, and my commitment to justice spoke to ordinary people who were also seekers on the journey. My study of scripture helped me to break open gospel stories in a contemporary context, bringing them to life and highlighting ways in which we could make a difference in our world by being authentic "doers" of the word of God, not just preachers or believers. I was a natural storyteller and I married this gift with my love of God, expressed through my storytelling. My own experiences with the VMM, in the desert, and on the streets of Chicago helped give my words a firm and practical foundation.

As I entered more intensively into the role of mothering I came to believe with a deep conviction that God was also Mother. This came about because I was so conscious that, in spite of the struggles and difficulties, my love for my child was so deep that I would give all for him—even die for him. I began to realize that this must be how God must feel for me and for all of us . . . that God loves us with such a passion (and I had experienced that passion) that we were inseparable. It was then that I began to refer to the Motherhood of God. There was no question that all the feminine qualities and all the nurturing qualities that I experience as a woman come from God and are of God. There was no doubt that the overwhelming experience I had had of God in the Sahara, in the trailer, and in the cabin in Pennsylvania—was strongly, powerfully, feminine. What I did not realize at this time was what a huge problem this would present to the men who were in leadership positions in my Church.

In 1993 I was invited to be a keynote speaker at Call To Action—a reform movement within the Catholic Church. I was also asked if I would participate in the liturgy to be attended by approximately three thousand priests, sisters and laity. This was no problem for me—I had been leading liturgical services and breaking bread for more than thirty years! (One could do this without saying the actual words of consecration which, according to the law of the Church were "for the priest alone.") The gatherings around bread and wine, gatherings of which I had been a part from the foundation of the VMM way back in the 1960s and 1970s had their origin in the early Church which celebrated *Agape*. Groups of Christians would gather to pray, to celebrate their faith and friendship, and to break bread as a sign of that faith and friendship and in memory of Jesus. We were not talking about the traditional Catholic concept of "transubstantiation" here—the belief that through the words of a male priest the bread and wine became the actual body and blood of Christ. As laity, we never claimed or declared that we were transforming the bread and wine into anything more than bread and wine—a symbol of fellowship and love. Our celebrations were also based on the belief that "wherever two or three are gathered in my name, there I am among them."

I never imagined therefore, that there would be a problem as I stood by the priest at the side of the altar. The celebration was held in a large banquet hall in which groups of people sat around tables. On each table there was a loaf of bread and a chalice of wine. The priest and I stood by the elevated altar. I had been asked to ritually place a stole on the priest, and he did the same for me. Wearing a stole was no big deal for me—it was simply a sign of being involved in a community gathered to pray and to worship. I never, for an instant, presumed myself to be garbed as a priest! Perhaps it should be noted here that my particular "stole" was utterly simple—it was burlap (sackcloth) and had been made by a group of children in their craft class. The children had glued acorns and leaves to the burlap as a symbol of the fall season. The thought that I should refuse to wear the stole never even occurred to me. In fact, rejecting the gift the children had made for me would not only have been discourteous—it would have made no sense.

When the time came for the Consecration, the presider invited everyone present—all three thousand people—to raise their hands and to hold up the bread and the wine. The presider then turned to me, handed me the chalice, and indicated that I should raise it. As I did so, a camera flashed.

This was the beginning of my being banned with increasing frequency and right up to the present time from some Catholic dioceses throughout the United States and even beyond. The photograph of me wearing a stole, standing by the altar, and holding up the chalice was published in the Catholic press a few days later with a caption stating that I had "presided at the liturgy." Publication of the picture was immediately followed by phone call after phone call cancelling my future speaking engagements and retreats in dioceses all over the country. I was branded, from that time on, as a dissident.

I was devastated.

In the years that followed I was taped, photographed, misquoted, and subjected to protests and angry letters from all sides. My writings were scrutinized and any reference to the feminine Divine or the Motherhood of God was used as a reason to bar me from my ministry of public speaking. Statements I had made were quoted out of context, censorious articles were written about me, and comments were posted on the Internet misrepresenting my spirituality and branding me a heretic.

I fled to The House of Sophia. I fled to hide in God's Womb.

> I will squirrel my pain away
> like a little hard nut
> and hide it deep in my guts
> until it is ready—
> having been warmed and softened
> in my belly—
> to break open
> and break down
> into little crumbs

which I will toss to the winds
to be carried far from me
into the universe
where my little pain
will forever circle—
as tiny dots in the cosmos—
taking its place
in the tattered and glorious trail
of the human story.

Sometimes,
like right now,
I know I am too fragile
to feel,
lest I just crumble
and fall
into so many pieces
I would never be able
to gather them all up.
Some might stay hidden,
never to be found,
leaving me
forever incomplete.
Better just to breathe deeply,
to stay intact,

until I am strong enough
to grieve
with dignity.

I lit a candle
to warm the cold
that clung around my heart,
a cold which, unbidden,
creeps around me
in moments unguarded,
leaving me
naked and so vulnerable
to the icy impact
of intended hurt.
But I must not die,
and this heart—
once so hot
and swelled with love—
must heal itself of assaults
that broke it up
and left it shivering
and betrayed.
I light a candle
and a thousand more, until,
in their fiery blaze,
I am a little comforted.

I walked, oh, so slowly
through the woods,
hearing the twigs beneath my feet
crack
like my heart breaking open,
and conscious
of the running stream
flowing like my tears.
"Let something good
happen in my life,"
I whispered to the air
elusive, intangible.
"Let something good
happen in my life"...
Then my eyes caught
the shining purple
of wild flowers
clustering in the grass,
looking at me,
demanding admiration
at the perfection
of their beauty.
And a bird
began to sing,
lone and sweet, in the branches

that swayed above me
like a canopy—
protective and gentle.
Then all at once
I saw
the earth, its waters,
stones and dazzling colors
rise up,
surrounding me
in a great green embrace
of comfort
calling my spirit to whisper
softly,
"Something good,
something good,
is happening in my life."

Why have you led me,
faithful God,
down paths so strewn
with treacherous rocks?
Why seduce me,
numbly praying,
into caverns of emptiness,
to tread on shards of glass?
Why, faithful God,

have you brought me here
to stand alone
declaring your Name
in dark and empty spaces,
echoing back to me
your passionate song of love?
Why, faithful God,
have you led me dancing
to your door
without a choir or music?
Why, faithful God,
have you dared to teach me,
wild and unashamed,
such a lonely dance
of love?

And then
the answer came,
so subtle
and so thunderous,
"Because, beloved,
you were there."

I came to an understanding:

"All that you have done, and all that has been done to you, is for your becoming."

In the past few years I have focused on women's retreats, sharing with thousands of women all over the country my belief in a compassionate, all-embracing God who is male as well as female. Because of my experiences on the streets of Chicago, and because of my conviction that God is passionate about the marginalized (e.g., prostitutes, gay people, homeless people, transgendered people, etc.) I know that God welcomes all people and that there is something of all God's creation in God's own Self. God therefore embraces white and black, male and female, straight and gay. God is all—and none—of these because God is unfathomable. I believe that the deeper we enter into the journey, the bigger God becomes—until we reach the stage where we no longer have any names or definitions for God.

God is.

We can only stand in awe before God's amazing love:

> Ah—Here's the God of love again!
> Eternally blind to sin,
> cheering and clapping at Heaven's gate
> ushering the sinners in.

I share this understanding with a passion, only because of my own journey on which I have struggled for so long to be faithful. I cannot but speak the truth that flows from my inner understanding.

That inner understanding is simply this: that God's love is far beyond our comprehension. We cannot even begin to sound the depth and breadth of this love for each single one of us and for all of creation. It is a love that takes precedence over all else, and must be fundamental to our call as Christians. This, I believe, was the message of Jesus and one which, clearly, we seem to be having a hard time embracing.

My journey has now led me into a space of valleys and boulders where, more and more, I face exclusion from doing that which I feel most called to do—to speak to the People of God, to share my faith, my experiences and my stories of God. There is no doubt about the reality of a deep spiritual hunger within humanity. We are all seeking that which, for the most part, we do not know. When one stumbles upon a God who longs to feed God's people, a God who yearns to comfort and to love, a God who, amazingly, calls us to be part of a great spiritual birthing, one is impelled to share that consciousness. This is how I feel. This journey was chosen for me. This journey continues to feed my hunger for God and lead me to a deepening consciousness that we can never name or define who or what this God is.

The great Christian mystic Meister Eckhart wrote that "We are all called to be mothers of God." Indeed, we are all called to birth something of God in our world. But our Church's focus on physical virginity rather than motherhood has led to a not-so-subtle dismissal of the blessing and grace of birthing and mothering and the spiritual power of virginity in terms of its potential for fruitfulness. If there is to be fruitfulness in one's life there must first be vulnerability and expectancy. All revelations come from God.

The insights and revelations I have received on this journey have been gratuitous—pure gift from God. I am impelled to speak the truth in my heart. But I am a woman, and the Church that I love has a problem—a serious problem—with the feminine. This is a huge mistake—indeed it is simply wrong, even sinful. It results in the exclusion and marginalization of over 50 percent of God's people from full and active participation in the Church's expression of its faith through ritual and the gifts of the Holy Spirit. The Church dares to ignore or dismiss the gifts of the Holy Spirit which have been freely given to women as well as to men. These gifts are desperately needed by our hungry people and by all who are searching.

There is such a fear of the feminine in the Catholic Church that some bishops have cancelled my retreats and missions in their dioceses based on their reading of articles that contain no truth, have no validity, or are simply expressions of hearsay and rumors that I am a threat to the faith of the people(!). Several of these articles cast me as a witch and a heretic. I am deeply saddened and, once again, I feel isolated and abandoned.

But I remember the words I heard in the Sahara:

> "It is my love of which you must speak—not my power or glory, not my might and majesty—but only of my love . . . My Spirit is within you . . . Do not be

afraid. Be steadfast. For I am with you. I have always been with you. I have loved you and now I send you . . . You are not alone. Speak in my Name."

I will go before you,
like a butterfly
filled with nectar
I will be waiting
and hovering
at your door.

I am deeply comforted.
I will continue to speak and write.

I got into this love affair with God
when I was a dreamer
and too young to know
that it would seduce and seize me
all of my life.
It led me dancing
on the mountaintops—
solitary and splendid.
It led me to vast and empty plains—
lonely and silent.
To grubby city streets—
hot and alive.
And to forests—
thick and dark.

This love affair
left a great imprint
on my soul—
un-erasable.
I did not know—
oh, I did not understand,
when I was yet a child—
that this wild God
would claim all,
without remorse or apology.
And I am left, now,
forever possessed.

CHAPTER THIRTEEN

THE ANSWER

At the beginning of this book I cited the question frequently asked of me: "Why are you still a member of the Catholic Church?" And I wrote that I could not answer that question in a few sentences—that I could answer it only through a reflection on my life's experiences.

I continue to be a member of my Church precisely because it is my Church. It is my identity—it is who I am. I cannot separate the Church from my personhood and from my journey with God. When Call To Action asked me in 2008 to address the question: "Why stay in the Roman Catholic Church?" I read the following story to the audience:

> Once upon a time there was a little girl who had a very special and exciting secret. She knew that her secret had to be kept, because if people heard about it, they might think she was a little odd and, certainly, a little different! Because, you see, the little

girl had discovered a great Mystery that filled her with deep peace and joy.

She had found it in a dark place—a huge old cathedral which sat on a hill overlooking her town in England. Every day the little girl would run into the great building and creep up to the altar, which was surrounded by paintings of angels with huge gold wings. There were flowers and candles everywhere and a sweet musky smell in the air. It was very, very beautiful. But, best of all, the little girl met her secret Friend in the shadows of the great cathedral and for hours they would just look at each other, and sometimes they would talk and make all sorts of promises to one another.

The little girl fell in love with her secret Friend, and the house where they met became her most *favorite* place in the whole world. In fact, it became HER house too. So the little girl promised she would never leave. And she knew she would not.

The little girl grew up and became old enough to begin to fulfill some of the promises she had made to her special Friend in their secret meeting place. She had promised God (for this is who her secret Friend *was*) that she would go to Africa to tell people all about God and the big house where they had met and fallen in love. The little girl always kept her promises, so, as soon as she could, she set off for a village in Africa.

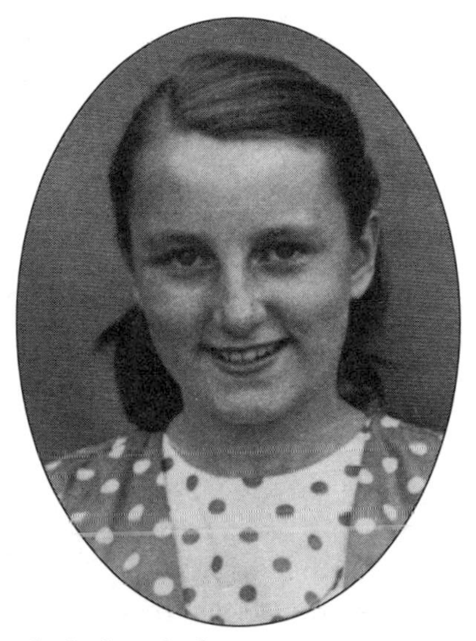

The little girl who never went away.

She lived with the villagers for three years. They were very poor, and even though she had gone to help *them* and tell them all about her special Friend and the big house, they taught HER things too! They had a HUGE spirit of hospitality and kindness. Even though the woman was a different color and culture and couldn't *even* speak their language (!), they welcomed her and took care of her and loved her. The woman began to realize that through these poor and different people God was teaching her more about what *God* must be like! She learned that the house where she had fallen in love with God must *also* welcome and love all people—even though they were different!

It looked like God's house needed to be REALLY BIG!

The woman was excited about this and about all the things the African people had taught her about God and about how much bigger God's house needed to be. She went back to her own people to tell the chief keeper of God's house (who was called a *bishop*) all about her experiences.

The woman pleaded with the keeper to let her speak in her Friend's house (the big cathedral) on Sunday to tell all the people what she had learned. This was the very house where she had first fallen in love with her secret Friend so she knew, deep down, that it was her house too. (But she did not tell the keeper that—she just knew it in her heart.)

The keeper told her that she *could* talk in her Friend's house, but that she must not wear pants—she was to wear a long skirt. She was also told to wear a mantilla to cover her head. The woman had never worn that in all her other visits to her Friend's house. So she told the keeper that she would wear a skirt but not a mantilla. The keeper seemed very worried...

On that special Sunday, as the woman stepped up to the altar (where she and God had spent so much time together), the keeper (who had decided to come and listen and sat in a special high chair in the middle) leaned over to her and whispered:

"Make it quick!" He said this to her as she walked in front of him toward the big pulpit where she was to stand and speak.

This really threw the woman and made her very nervous, even though she was in her own house with her special Friend, and even though she knew every angel wing and every candle, and every corner, and every cranny. The keeper's words made her freeze.

The woman climbed up into the big pulpit and saw the hundreds of faces looking up at her. And she couldn't say a word—not even a quick one ...So she just stood there all frozen up. And she knew the keeper was watching her. Then all of a sudden it seemed as if all the people in her Friend's house were sending waves of light and joy to her. They were smiling and nodding, and the woman knew that her Friend was there too—nodding and smiling. So she opened her mouth and began to speak. Even though the keeper had told her to make it quick, she didn't, because all the people kept on smiling and nodding.

After that (which took place more than forty years ago) the keeper told her that she couldn't talk in the house anymore and that she had to keep quiet about her special Friend and stop telling people that God had a big house.

So the woman thought it would be good to get more people to go to Africa and poor countries in order to discover for *themselves* that God was big and that God's house must be big too. She started a movement called the Volunteer Missionary Movement (VMM), which sent more than two thousand lay people to places all around the world over the next thirty-five years. The woman knew that it was important for as many people as possible to learn about God being so big—even though the people from whom they learned were of different colors and spoke in different languages. (Also, she always kept her promises, and one of them was always to listen to her heart.)

Then the woman's special Friend sent her off to a different country called America. The woman wasn't too happy about that. She missed her family and her own country but she knew that God's house was SO big that her Friend wanted her to meet even more strange people and invite *them* to the big house! It was really hard for the woman to understand all the demands her lifelong Friend was making of her, so she hid in a forest for nine months. She had to listen really hard to make sure she was getting the message right.

But yes, she *was* getting the message right (even though her Friend *whispered* a lot); she heard it really well. God told her that all the different people God had made were really special and precious no matter who they were or what they had done—

God wanted to invite them *all* to God's big house. There was enough room for everybody—and lots of food too!

So the woman went off and told the prostitutes, the drug addicts, the winos, the homeless—and even the Catholics (!) that they *all* had a place in her Friend's house which was HUGE! She also told them that God was ecstatic about ALL of them.

Through the woman's experience she came to know that her Friend was really like a BIG MOTHER who loved absolutely everyone. So she started talking about that too. (That REALLY got her into a lot of trouble!)

The keepers weren't at all sure that the woman had got that message right, but *she* knew that she had listened *really* well and also that she knew her Friend pretty well too. Anyway, she told the keepers (and even wrote it down!) that her Friend loved everybody and even forgave them and would give them food—whether they were sorry or not!

After that, things began to get more difficult—especially when the woman ran into people who were REALLY DIFFERENT—like Protestants and gay people and EVEN women like herself! The keepers made rules about the different people and they told the woman that they weren't all welcome in her Friend's house, and especially that they could not have any food in the house.

But the woman remembered that her Friend had told her that there was enough food for everybody. She had also been told that everybody had been made as they *were meant to be* and that none of God's people had been made "disordered" (as some of the keepers were saying). Her Friend was VERY emphatic about that!

The keepers also reminded her that she was a *woman* and so she couldn't talk in her Friend's house anymore—even though she had actually been doing that for more than forty years! The woman could not understand this . . . and neither could her special Friend who had taught her so much about what to say . . .

At first the woman got mad. Then she cried. Then she went off to the woods again to hide and to meet with her special Friend (who always turned up in the woods nowadays even more than in the big house!). But she had promised that she would never leave her Friend's house—even if things got rough.

In the woods her Friend told her that some of the keepers had forgotten how big the house was and that God's *own boy* (who was called Jesus) had told them AGES ago to leave the door open and the light on. (The woman had heard that even Motel 6 did that.) She was baffled as to why these keepers did not do what even Motel 6 did to welcome people! When she mentioned this to them they got REALLY cross and told her she should go find another house. But she wouldn't, because she loved the house where she had first met and come to know her special Friend. (Also, she always kept her promises.)

The woman kept on talking to lots of other people about God and she listened to how sad and hurt they were feeling because of the keepers who were asking for special IDs at God's house and keeping all sorts of people out. Then these keepers started calling the woman names and saying unkind and untrue things about her. But the worst thing was that they started to close the door *shut* whenever they saw her coming. In fact, they began to lock it!

The woman felt her heart begin to break. But she also knew that her special Friend's heart was breaking too. She knew that the house *belonged to her Friend* and that no one else—not even the keepers—had any right to say that *they owned it*. The woman knew that she could never go away and leave God's house to the keepers even though (and maybe even because they REALLY, REALLY wanted her to go away!).

So the woman began to study about other women who had lived hundreds of years ago, women who were called Beguines. They had also discovered the special Friend in the silence of their hearts. Like the woman, they too got so excited that they told ordinary women and men (who were not even keepers but were called laity) what God was like and that God wanted all of them to share the big house and the food that was waiting. They were very brave women, because they knew that they could be imprisoned and even killed for talking and writing about God and God's big house.

The woman began to pray to these women who had had similar problems. She found new courage and strength. She decided that she would not leave her Friend's house... at least not yet... for she remembered all the times she and her Friend had talked and played and loved in the house and how she had promised never to leave. She also would stay to honor the memory of her sisters who had suffered so much or been killed for what they really believed.

But she also knew that, if the time should ever come when her *special Friend* could not get into the house because it had become so small, then that would be the time when they would both have to leave because there would be no room anymore. She knew that then the door would be completely shut even to God and all God's special friends and that *then* the light would surely be completely out. It would be dark...

The shadows were already lengthening...

But she was used to the dark—because it was in the darkness of the cathedral, God's big house, that they had first met and become such good, good friends. She would stay to try to keep the light on and the door ajar...

She knew that her special Friend loved the house and loved the keepers too!

So her special Friend would not be ready to leave until the light was completely out and the door was tightly shut.

Then, she knew, they would leave *together*.

And head, maybe, for Motel 6.

CONCLUSION

The story of the little girl and her secret Friend was told from a place of pain, a place of longing that we, the People of God, might become more conscious of God's immeasurable and unconditional love for each one of us. It's a lesson all of us need to learn and learn again throughout our lives. "Unconditional" is difficult for us to comprehend because it demands total forgiveness and acceptance. This is huge. This is a challenge. This is unreasonable! But so, I believe, is God, whose love is beyond our comprehension.

This is the challenge of my life and what I endeavor to teach and continue to learn. As I noted in the Introduction, it is a challenge that comes not from books and not from me, but from the grace of God that moves each one of us in directions that God chooses for us whether we are conscious of it or not.

Our spiritual journey is an ongoing response to a divine seduction. We ourselves are to become more like the Great Lover. This journey, therefore, will be fraught with pain and struggle as our egos resist the divine invitation. We all resist in one way or another. We do not want to get hurt. But, as someone once wrote, "It is the crack in your heart that lets the Mystery in." We all have a crack in our hearts; we have all been hurt, offended, rejected, dismissed—every one of us, in one way or another. But it is that very crack that can open us up to what this journey is all about—*the call to love one another*—no matter what. We must rise up, again and again, to continue stumbling faithfully toward God.

I remember the words I heard in the solitude and silence of the Sahara:

> "I am faithful . . . I am love . . . It is my love of which you must speak."

No one is to be excluded from this love. No matter how difficult the terrain, we must continue the journey. As we do so in faithfulness, God gets bigger and we become oh, so much smaller! But in that process we also become deeply conscious of the amazing presence of God . . .

For God
(we are to discover)
is right here,
around us,
above,
below,

behind,
and before . . .
soaked in our reality.
And we are oh,
so, so comforted.

At the beginning of this book there is a poem called "The Cathedral" that describes the awe I felt in my youth before the mystery of God. Now, at the end of this book, I write about another experience of cathedral. And this one leaves me not so much now in awe as in deep, deep gratitude.

Another Cathedral

Here—
in this great green cathedral—
there are no angels' wings
sweeping in gold curves
around raised altar.
Here, too,
there are no gilded arches
or marble pillars
rising into lofty darkness
upholding
ornate ceiling
shining with painted saints.
Oh, no,
here now in this great cathedral
I sit upon
an old wooden bench
half grey—blanched by the sun,
half red—curling with
blistered paint.
And all around
I am assailed
by the songs of birds,
sweeter than any choir,
trilling in wild

unbridled joy
at life.
No priest stands here—
hands outstretched,
clad in flowing robes.
Only trees raise up
their branches,
thick with blossoms,
proclaiming the work
of God.
No little boys,
robed in white lace,
process around this space—
only rabbits and chipmunks
run oblivious and joyous
upon this sacred ground.
No incense smell wafts
in mysterious clouds
from gold ciborium,
but I feel the gentle kiss
of the breeze,
carrying with it
the scent of wildflowers—
and dogwood blossom
sweetening all my senses.
And above me,
spanning all of nature's loveliness,

the dome of the sky
hangs over all
and every scudding cloud
pretends
it is an angel.
Here in this great green cathedral
I am no longer a child
Awestruck,
as once I was,
by the mystery of God.
Ah, now I am a woman,
blanched a little grey,
like this bench,
and curling at the edges.
I sit in this
abandoned and splendid place
soaked now,
not in awe,
but in wisdom
born of journeying,
long and dark
though pierced through with shafts
of radiant light,
revealing
my soul's longing,
deep and true,
for the God

Who breathes—
ah,
so deeply
here
in *this*
great green cathedral.

Alleluia!
Amen!

Also by Edwina Gateley

Soul Sisters

Women in Scripture Speak to Women Today
by Edwina Gateley,
Art by Louis Glanzman

ISBN 978-1-57075-443-2

Catholic Press Association Award Winner

Poet Edwina Gateley joins with artist Louis Glanzman to reveal the souls of women loved by Jesus.

"When I first saw Louis Glanzman's paintings of twelve women in the gospels whose names are so familiar, something happened inside me. After a lifetime of knowing all about these women I felt, at last, that I had actually met them. Indeed I had. They were people I already knew: homemakers, sex workers, child runaways, crones, teachers, mothers, senior citizens . . . all of them knew Jesus. All of them were archetypes who reflected the journeys, struggles, joys and dreams of women today."

—Edwina Gateley

Christ in the Margins

by Robert Lentz, Edwina Gateley

ISBN 978-1-57075-321-3

"Uplifting . . . exquisite . . . an ideal resource for those on a spiritual journey with its inspiring examples of mentors who worked for peace, justice, and transformation in adverse circumstances."

—*Spirituality & Health*

"Arresting . . . explores how Christ is revealed to us in the lives of men and women working at the margins of society . . . "

—*Saint Anthony Messenger*

Christ in the Margins features forty Robert Lentz icons and biographies of Christ-figures who confound the status quo. Together with Edwina Gateley's lyrical portraits of contemporary men and women who have revealed the Christ-presence to her in the most unlikely places, it is both profoundly spiritual and spiritually profound.

Thank you for reading *In God's Womb*. We hope you enjoyed it.